THE IMAGE OF MAN IN THE TORAH

PETER VAN 'T RIET

THE IMAGE OF MAN
IN THE TORA

CONTRIBUTION TO THE DEBATE ON
NORMS AND PRINCIPLES IN MODERN SOCIETY

FOLIANTI - KAMPEN 2018

Original title in Dutch: Het mensbeeld van de Tora
Published as a paper copy in 2006 by Uitgeverij Kok, Kampen. The Netherlands
and republished in 2014 by Folianti, Kampen, The Netherlands

Translated into English by Dick Broeren Sr
© Folianti, Kampen 2018 (paperback edition)
ISBN/EAN: 978-90-76783-49-9
NUR-code: 703 (Bible Sciences)

CONTENTS

CONTENTS

Introduction

"After all the horrors we experienced, we don't believe in God any longer, but we'll stick to his Torah." Some Jews, survivors of the German extermination camps, realized this, when they tried to pick up their lives after the end of World War II. Personally I know of only a few statements that better represent the paradoxical situation of modern believers, or perhaps one should say of modern man, than this one. For one thing we live in a world from which God is disappearing, a world that shows fantastic, but also disconcerting aspects. For another, we feel the need for a more authoritative "code of conduct and life" than the code of interhuman subjectivity only.

In this book *The Image of man in the Tora* I have tried to describe the "code of conduct and life" as Judaism has put into practice for centuries. The first five chapters show a selection from the many aspects of that image of man. The first chapter has an introductory character, the first version once started as a meditation for a base community. A Talmudic statement, rather freely translated with: "Three acts maintain the world: learning Torah, prayer and acts of friendship", was my inspiration for the subjects of the chapters 2, 3 and 4. They deal successively with: man as a learning being; man reflecting on himself and on his relation with God and his fellow man; and man as a socially-minded being. In chapter 5 the concept of 'shalom' comes up for discussion. Shalom, that is peace and welfare for all people, the fulfilment of the world. The image of man in the Torah intends to reach that aim.

It will be apparent that the image of man in the Torah as a code of conduct and life still has a lot to offer even today in the modern, globalizing society, in which all kinds of images of man often play a hidden part. That's why I couldn't resist comparing the image of man in the Torah with other images of man that strongly influence our western culture. In this context chapter 6 offers a concise discussion of the images of man in (orthodox) Christianity, Islam and various secular movements. This forced me to choose as well. In my view the image of man in the Torah offers today's man, whether Jew or Chistian, a middlecourse between on the one hand religious, enforced rules of the orthodox Christianity and the Islam, and on the other hand the multicoloured arbitrariness of the rationalistic and romantic philosophies of the past four centuries.

And therefore I hope that this study can and will make a positive contribution to the debate on norms and principles in our modern society.

Autumn 2018   Peter van 't Riet

1 The Image of Man in the Torah

The Torah – the first five books of the Bible – speaks about God. This, of course, can't be denied. Fat tomes have been filled with theology, the "knowledge of God" in the Torah, in which the authors tried to answer numerous questions about God. But reading the Bible, I, more often than not, can't help the feeling that God is taken for granted and that man is the real problem. That's the reason why I got fascinated by the question after the image of man in the Torah. And apparently this question could only be answered by reading the Torah in the light of the old rabbinical exegesis. Their language and their line of thought are most cognate to the Torah.

In this introductory chapter I'll discuss a number of aspects of the image of man in the Torah and I'll try to actualize them a little. A little, because I take the view that each reader ought to make his or her own actualization of what he or she finds valuable in this book. Almost every day I happen to find the image of man in the Torah surprisingly modern. Central notions like responsibility for the completion of the creation (the natural and human reality), learning all one's life, mending damaged relations, quality of life, organizing a just society: they are all notions that still play an important part in the social and ideological debate, even today. Man, who will turn out to be God's partner in the process of creation – more about that later on – needs, next to his own experience and intellect, the sounding board of the Torah in order to be able to find out what he ought and ought not to do in this world. Therefore it is useful – before discussing the image of man in the Torah – to think about a number of aspects of the Torah itself briefly: what, in fact, is the Torah and who is it meant for?

What is the Torah and who is it meant for?

To begin with, we could say, the Torah consists of the first five books of the Bible: Genesis, Exodus, Leviticus, Numbers and Deuteronomy. In Judaism these books are written in Hebrew in one scroll traditionally, one 'sefer torah', the reason why these five books are often called the 'written Torah'. In addition to this there is the so-called 'oral Torah'. The stories and rules in Genesis up to and including Deuteronomy have always been part of a much larger complex of stories and rules that were passed on orally as well. This oral Torah, for the greater part a real 'oral' tradition in the first centuries of the Christian Era (CE), was put into writing only later in anthologies such as the 'Mishnah' (until 200 CE), the Talmud[a] (until c. 500/600 CE) and the 'Midrash' (until far into the Middle Ages).[1]

All the same, these traditions are still called 'the oral Torah', even today. The oral Torah complements the written Torah, explains it and applies it to situations in life which raise new questions again and again. Without the oral Torah the written Torah can't be understood properly. The rabbis express the close connection between the written and the oral Torah by saying that both were given by God to Moses at Sinai. And the image of man stands out especially clear in the oral Torah.

Even the problem of whom the Torah is meant for would be solved from the oral Torah. After all, we could ask ourselves the question: if God gave the Torah to Moses at Sinai, it's only meant for the people of Israel, isn't it? And the other nations, have they anything to do with the Torah? The rabbis gave a clear answer to these questions in the oral Torah. However, they formulated the question a bit differently: "Why was the Torah given in the wilderness and why not in the land of Israel?" The answer is:[2] "The Torah was given in the wilderness, in

---

a   The Talmud is the most important after-biblical anthology of Judaism. There are two versions: the Jerusalem (jT) and the Babylonian (bT). The Talmud consists of the Mishnah and a large number of comments on the Mishnah, the Gêmara (final editing 500 and 600 CJ).

public, for everyone to see. If the Torah had been given in the land of Israel, the people of Israel could have said to the nations of the world: 'It is not for you'. That's why the Torah was given in the wilderness, in no man's land, publicly, visible for all. And all those who wish to receive the Torah can come and get it."

We already come across this universal attitude in the written Torah itself. A clear example is the covenant or partnership God makes with Noah (Genesis 9:1-19). It's not only a covenant or partnership with Noah, but a partnership with Noah and all his descendants (v. 9). And later in verse 12 we find a specifically Hebrew expression: "for all the generations of the olam". This can be translated in two ways: God makes with Noah an 'eternal' covenant with all generations, but he also makes a covenant with all generations 'of the world'. And in verse 13 it is repeated once more: 'a covenant between God and the earth'. We could say that here the Torah shows its meaning for all nations which, at least according to the Bible story, all descend from Noah. The later covenant between God and Israel at Sinai doesn't abolish this Noahide Covenant, but adds new obligations of partnership, especially meant for the people of Israel. The other nations could keep coming to no man's land Sinai – if they want to – and receive the Torah in their own Noahide way.[a]

Now a second question could be asked as well: Israel received the Torah about 3000 years ago according to the tradition. How then could this book still be a book for our times? All these old stories and all these old rules of life, could they have any meaning for modern people like us? And this, of course, isn't a question asked in our time only. Already centuries ago the rabbis answered this question in their own imaginative ways. They tell:[3] "When God wanted to give the Torah to Israel, the people gathered around Mount Sinai. The men were at the back, the women were in front and before them stood the pregnant

---

a At present it becomes increasingly clear in the Christian world that the meaning of Jesus of Nazareth is inextricably bound up with the fact that he was a Torah-abiding Jew. Therefore, it's necessary for Christians today to study the Torah as a source of faith.

13

women. As soon as God began to speak the pregnant women's bellies became transparent as glass, thus all later generations could experience this event and vouch for the Torah!" In other words: the Torah is given for all generations even today's.

Yet the question hasn't been answered what kind of book the Torah, with regards to its content, is in fact. Traditionally there is a false idea in Christianity about the Torah. Influenced by Greek and Latin translations the Hebrew word 'torah' is usually translated with 'Law'. A black-and-white definition of a law could be that it is a collection of strict rules: it is not a special merit to stick to them, but breaking the rules should be punished. The Torah however, is not a law in that specific sense. The Hebrew word 'torah' is derived from the verb 'jara', which means 'to point (to)', 'to teach' or 'to learn'. So a better translation for the word 'Torah' is 'Teachings' or 'Education'. The Torah should be taken as a textbook, from which you could learn how life is meant by God. In the first place the Torah describes how man should or should not live his life and how the society should or should not be organized, so that both the lives of man and of society should improve. The Torah should not be taken as a 'law', but rather as a 'constitution': the constitution of God's kingship over the world. That is why the Torah is a manifesto and not a random set of rules for life. The first word of the Torah shows this already. This first word of the book of Genesis is the Hebrew word 'bêreshit', usually translated with 'in the beginning'. But it could also be translated with 'in principle':[a] 'In principle God created the heavens and the earth'. And as a declaration of principles the Torah should be studied upon and elaborated so that her rules and laws could be applied to the day-to-day life.

So the Torah is a declaration of principles. The rabbis tell that God, when he created the world, created the Torah first. And then, reading the Torah, he created the world.[4] In other words: the Torah is the design, the 'charcoal drawing' for the creation. Consequently, the

---

a   The word 'bêreshit' is cognate with the Hebrew word 'rosh', meaning 'head' or 'beginning'. So it could be translated with 'in a beginning', but also with 'in principle' or 'principally'.

Torah is also the instrument God used and still uses to create the world. At Mount Sinai God gave the Torah, this instrument to create the world with, to Israel first and in Israel to mankind. Thus man became God's partner in the process of creation and could use the Torah as an instrument to help perfecting the creation as meant by God.[a, 5]

However, the Torah doesn't describe meticulously how to do this. It is after all a declaration of principles, a constitution, that should be applied and elaborated again and again in each new situation. The exegesis of the Torah, its application to all spheres of life, is a matter of individual believers and of the community of faith itself. No heavenly voices even crop up in after-biblical times/days, so the rabbis say, let alone popes or synods that think they're allowed to speak backed by the authority of heaven.[6] One can imagine that this is accompanied by an image of man that differs completely from the image of man that dominated the Christian tradition for centuries.[b] And this other image of man implies another notion of the relation between God and man as well. In this chapter I'll discuss some aspects of the image of man in the Torah and in the next chapters I'll go more deeply into some important aspects of it.

Man as God's Partner

Psalm 8 can be read as a poetic summary of how the Bible looks at man in his relation to God:[c]

O LORD, our Lord,
How excellent is Your name in all the earth,
Who have set Your glory above the heavens!
Out of the mouth of babes and nursing infants

---

a   We'll meet this thought again towards the end of the Torah in
    Deuteronomy 30.
b   I'll return to that in chapter 6.
c   NKJV Bible.

You have ordained strength,
Because of Your enemies,
That You may silence the enemy and the avenger.
When I consider Your heavens, the work of Your fingers,
The moon and the stars, which You have ordained,
What is man that You are mindful of him,
And the son of man that You visit him?
For You have made him a little lower than the angels,
And You have crowned him with glory and honour.
You have made him to have dominion over the works of Your
    hands;
You have put all things under his feet,
All sheep and oxen —
Even the beasts of the field,
The birds of the air,
And the fish of the sea
That pass through the paths of the seas.

O LORD, our Lord,
How excellent is Your name in all the earth!

This is a song of praise of someone who discovered that he is God's partner in the creation. The first pages of the Torah already speak clearly and unambiguously of the partnership between God and man. In the first chapter of Genesis God is busily creating and creating, and He creates man 'in His image, according to His likeness'. That can only mean that man is being created as 'co-creator'. And lo and behold! Having created this co-creator God can stop creating for a full day and leave his creation alone! Only then God can create the 'sabbath', the day God and man will observe together without working. The day that is called in Judaism 'the day of the world to come', a world created by God and man together.

This vision on man is closely connected with how the Torah writes about God. The thought that God created man in his image can be worded in a more modern way: to create man God uses himself as an example. The use of such images for God and his activities often makes theologists suppose that the Bible shows an anthropomorphic image of God, an image of God looking like a man. As they say: the Bible uses inadequate human images to be able to write about God. However, this notion is not correct. It has its origins in a Greek-philosophical outlook on God. God is in the eyes of the Greek philosophers so exalted, so supermundane, so incomprehensible, such an Unmoved Mover, that it's almost impossible to speak about him in common terms. Yet people want to speak about him and eventually they use terms derived from daily human life. Hence the anthropomorphic image of God.

In the Torah however, it's just the other way round. The Torah knows a 'theomorphic image of man' rather than an anthropomorphic image of God and speaks about man in terms derived from God. That is to say, shaping his life man should use God as the model He is. That is the meaning of 'created in his image'. That's also the reason the Bible doesn't have any theology, no science of God, it's rather an anthropological book.[a, 7] Judaism could be called, in a sense that is, an anthropological religion. Nowhere in Torah there is a 'god-problem', but she shows a 'man-problem' in almost every page. God is always entirely taken for granted, man not by any manner or means. This theomorphic image of man is repeatedly worded in the often repeated, divine order to man: 'You shall be holy, for I the LORD your God am holy' (Leviticus 19,2; 20,26). In other words: <u>differ</u> (from other nations), because I <u>differ</u> (from the other Gods). After all, that's the meaning of the word 'holy'. In the Torah the actions of God are the very examples for the actions of man.

The actions of God as an example for human conduct is a central theme in the rabbis' exegesis of the Torah. Some examples. They ask

---

a   The Jewish scholar Abraham Joshua Heschel (1907-1972) once wrote that the Bible doesn't contain any human theology (an anthropomorphic image of God) and so doesn't give opinions about God from the human point of view, but presents instead a divine anthropology (a theomorphic image of man). So the Bible doesn't look at God from the human point of view, but looks at man from the God-point of view (see endnote).

for instance the question why God had made only one human being and not a multitude of them. The answers to this question went into all kinds of directions. One of these answers emphasizes the value of each and every human life: 'Therefore, only one human being was created to teach you that everyone who destroys one single human life, destroys an entire world; however, everyone who saves one single human life, saves an entire world'. This means for the conduct of man that essentially one should deal with the life of one's fellow man as if the survival of the entire world depends on it. Another answer to the same question underscores the fundamental unity and equality of all men: 'For the sake of peace among them God created one single man, so that no one can say to another: My father was more important than yours.' A third answer does not only voice the greatness of the Holy One – praised be He – but wants to emphasize man's individuality:[8] 'When someone strikes several coins with the same die, they will all be the same. However, the King of kings, the Holy One – praised be He – coins each individual man with the die of the first Adam and none of them is equal to the others.' And the Talmud continues: 'That's why every man should say: the world was created for my sake.' Everyone's individual responsibility for the world and for his or her fellow man stems from that knowledge.

Following God's example could be called 'the imitation of God', the 'imitatio Dei'.[a] Plenty examples can be found in the Talmud and in the Midrash of how the rabbis explain the actions of God as examples of conduct for man. One could imagine that the essential fact of man as the image of God, as co-creator and jointly responsible for the world, leads to an optimistic outlook on mankind. Man was created – just like the rest of the creation – well: 'tov', 'okay', as the Hebrew text of Gene-

---

a   Christianity knows since Thomas of Aquino (1224-1274) the so-called 'imitatio Christi', or 'Imitation of Christ'. Even though this 'Imitation of Christ' is motivated differently in orthodox-Christian theology, it could be transformed – within the Jewish re-interpretation of the New Testament – into the Torah's more radical 'imitatio Dei'. After all, Jesus represents in the gospels the figure of the messianic man who fully realizes the fact that he is created in the image of God.

sis 1 goes. But of course, the next question will be: what about evil and sin in the world?

Free Choice

At the end of Torah a manisfesto, a declaration of principles, is found about the free will and free choice for man: 'I call heaven and earth as witnesses today against you, that I have set before you life and death, blessing and cursing; therefore choose life, that both you and your descendants may live' (Deuteronomy 30:19, NKJV). Striking about this text is that this free choice is made individually, but certainly by an individual within the community. And it is striking as well that the consequences of everyone's choice for future generations are mentioned. Man is free in his or her choice, but this is always made within the community and with consequences for the community.

As we already saw earlier, man was created 'tov', that is 'well' or 'okay'. But that doesn't mean that he, as a servile soul, was only predestined to do good. He is – and that is 'tov' as well – equipped with two inclinations or possibilities: the inclination to do good (Hebrew: 'jétsèr ha-tov') and the inclination to do wrong ('jétsèr ha-ra').[9] Indeed, man is urged to do good emphatically, as could be read in Deuteronomy 30, but – and that is of the utmost importance for Torah – man is free to choose which of both inclinations or possibilities he wants to follow. What does it mean for coping with the evil inclination?

When in paradise Eve and the serpent talk to each other (Genesis 3), then in the Midrash the serpent isn't as much as a mythical creature, but Eve's own evil inclination. Eve is the first who dares to confront the 'jétsèr ha-ra', the evil inclination, and in doing so causes man to reach maturity.[a] She's the first human being who dares to explore the consequences of complying with the evil inclination. Fighting down, or even stamping out the evil inclination is not the issue here – how could one, being born with it -, it boils down especially to being

---

a   The Jewish tradition is more positive about Eve's part than the Christian tradition.

able to live with the evil inclination, to recognize it in yourself, to learn to control it[a] and even to learn to use it for the better.[10]

This can only be done by means of a learning process in which the Torah, the divine doctrine for human conduct, plays the central part. Without the Torah, such a learning process won't be possible. After all, if our attitude in life would exclusively be based on our own ideas of good and evil, we'll quickly think that all our actions – the not so pretty ones included – are in order and can be justified.[11] The Torah, however, rejects and tries to turn back this law of the jungle.[12] 'You shall neither mistreat a stranger nor oppress him, for you were strangers in the land of Egypt. You shall not afflict any widow or fatherless child' (Exodus 22:20-21).

The Torah aims to elevate the evil inclination, the lowest, animal instincts of man, above the everyday things of life, and to apply it for spiritual growth and a dignified existence.[13] The learning process needed, is a process by trial and error. But a failure is no reason to be taken aback. One of the greatest Jewish scholars, Abraham Joshua Heschel once said:[14] 'Jews have learned traditionally to enjoy themselves more about the fact that they will be able to fulfil Torah, albeit imperfectly, than worry about the fact that they won't be able to fulfil it perfectly.' Besides, the Torah equips us with the methods how to deal with our failures.

Someone who wants to learn from the Torah how to live, can learn to change his evil inclination into good actions. Who feels greedy, can learn to be generous. Who feels ambitious, can learn to adopt a modest attitude in company and to praise others. Who is inclined to speak ill, can learn to protect his fellow man against others. Who senses vindictiveness in himself can learn to make an effort to realize a proper judicial procedure. Of course one can wonder whether all this isn't a

---

a   Next advice is a case in point: 'If you walk past a brothel each day going to your work or returning home, walk around the block every day, because you should never say to yourself: this shall never happen to me.' I wrote this down by the end of the seventies in the study-house of Will J. Barnard (1923-1993). Up to now I've not been able to retrieve whether this statement is derived from rabbinic literature.

licence to insincerity, and whether this would produce distorted personalities. The Jewish tradition, however, teaches us that this needn't be the case, if one goes through one's own learning process consciously and patiently. Of course, one should prefer good actions that issue from positive motives. But it's better to act well from wrong motives and inclinations, than to act wrong on bad grounds. In the first place Jewish thought is aimed at the actions of man and its moral quality. The faith, the motives that prompted these actions, are of minor importance. The rabbis even believe that acting well will be able to improve man's motives in the end. The more or less common idea that one shouldn't do any religious obligations, when one doesn't feel the need, is completely inconsistent with the image of man in the Torah. This is the idea of Judaism: perform your religious obligations, then the need will grow automatically.[15]

Sin isn't fate, it's an action

The Torah is a textbook from which one can learn to become a complete man. She hands us rules we can use when looking for better conduct. This raises the question what to do when the rules of the Torah are broken. Even in these cases the Torah tells us what to do, as illustrated by some rather strong examples from the book of Leviticus:

> Then the LORD spoke to Moses, saying: "If a person commits a trespass, and sins unintentionally in regard to the holy things of the LORD [i.e. things for the sacrificial service], then he shall bring to the LORD as his trespass offering a ram without blemish from the flocks. And he shall make restitution for the harm that he has done in regard to the holy thing, and shall add one-fifth to it and give it to the priest. So the priest shall make atonement for him with the ram of the trespass offering, and it shall be forgiven him" (Leviticus 5,14-16).

21

Such an approach is not only valid towards God, but also towards one's fellow man, because later we read:[a]

> "If a person sins and commits a trespass against the LORD by lying to his neighbour:
>
> - about what was delivered to him for safekeeping,
> - or about a pledge,
> - or about a robbery,
> - or if he has extorted from his neighbour,
> - or if he has found what was lost and lies concerning it,
> - or if he swears falsely in any one of these things that a man may do in which he sins
>
> then it shall be, because he has sinned and is guilty, that he shall restore [to his neighbour]:
>
> - what he has stolen,
> - or the thing which he has extorted,
> - or what was delivered to him for safekeeping,
> - or the lost thing which he found,
> - or all that about which he has sworn falsely.
>
> He shall restore its full value, add one-fifth more to it, and give it to whomever it belongs, on the day of his trespass offering. And he shall bring his trespass offering to the LORD, a ram without blemish from the flock [...] to the priest. So the priest shall make atonement for him before the LORD, and he shall be forgiven for any one of these things that he may have done in which he trespasses" (Leviticus 6,1-6).[b]

---

a   Because this is a full quotation, I've tried to clarify the structure by means of dashes.

b   NKJV. In some bible translations Leviticus 5:20-26.

These two texts are extraordinary instructive as far as the Torah's approach of breaking her rules are concerned. Therefore the next observations.

The Hebrew word, translated above with 'misbehave', is in the accepted translation usually rendered with the verb 'to sin'. So sin is wrong behaviour and as such an act and no fate of man. Sin as a fundamental characteristic of human existence – original sin – is a notion unknown to Torah and Judaism.[a] The Hebrew word for 'sin' is 'chattat'. It's a form of the verb 'chata', meaning 'to miss', 'to miss a target', 'to misbehave' or 'to do the wrong things'. It's not the quality of the situation man finds himself in that is that much important, but the quality of his conduct. Sin is an incorrect or wrong action done by man. So perhaps it's better to speak of 'misconduct' or 'misbehaviour', not necessarily of a crime.

Misbehaviour or misconduct always takes place in a relation and disturbs or breaks that relation. The texts from Leviticus mentioned above are clear examples. Misconduct can happen on purpose or accidentally, but in all cases someone bears responsibility for what he's done in that relation. He can be called to account by his partner or fellow man. And that responsibility means that he should restore the relation by dispelling his misconduct. The Torah shows in some cases how to do this, as we can see in both texts from Leviticus stated above. They show that the inflicted damage in the cases mentioned should be compensated completely. Besides, an additional satisfaction of one-fifth of the value should be given as well,[b] because the damage for the injured party has always been more than the original value only. And it's important too, that the height of the extra compensation in case of misconduct towards God is equal to the compensation towards man. In both cases 125 % of the original damage should be paid. Also one

---

a   The idea of 'original sin' doesn't happen in the Christian sources (the New Testament). It was developed by Church Fathers like Augustine of Hippo (354-430).

b   Following the rabbinical tradition, this one-fifth part of the finally granted amount is not 20% but 25% of the original value (the total amount). After all, this interpretation is clearly the most favourable for the beneficiary.

should compensate for the damage in both cases first, and only then forgiveness and atonement by means of a guilt-offering will be possible.

Another issue is to be derived from the second part of the text. Bad actions towards one's fellow man not only disturb the relation with that fellow man, but also the relation with God and so both should be repaired forthwith. And – in doing so – it is imperative to observe the order: first the relation with one's fellow man should be repaired, only then one should endeavour to repair the relation with God. This principle plays an important part in Judaism, for instance during the ten days prior to 'Yom Kippur', the Day of Atonement. During the Day of Atonement only misconduct towards God is reconciled. Man should repair his misconduct towards his fellow man during the ten days, the so-called Days of Awe, preceding the Day of Atonement, because otherwise the Day of Atonement won't result in atonement with God. In the New Testament Jesus expresses the same Torah-principle in the Sermon on the Mount as well:

> Therefore if you bring your gift to the altar, and there remember that your brother has something against you, leave your gift there before the altar, and go your way. First be reconciled to your brother, and then come and offer your gift (Matthew 5:23-24).

The responsibility for one's own misconduct is so big that it's forbidden to grant someone forgiveness, who doesn't ask for it him/herself. The oral Torah compares it with killing the other person.[a] Who grants his fellow man forgiveness without asking him for it, doesn't treat him as a responsible human being any more. In that case one deprives the

---

a   See for instance the archetypal story in bT Yoma 87a about the disturbed relation between Rav (3rd century) and the butcher. Rav sets out on the day before the Day of Atonement to try to make the butcher see the error of his ways, but his student Rabbi Huna is of the opinion that by doing so he will kill the butcher. And indeed, the story ends with the death of the unrepentant butcher.

other person of the most essential aspect of being human: being some-one in the image of God, being a partner in his creation.

Man's Task

As seen above, the first chapter of the book of Genesis tells us that 'in principle' God created the heavens and the earth. But that doesn't mean that the work was done, was finished, that the world was com-pleted. So God created man at the beginning of the creation but not mankind as a whole, indeed man and woman, but not the nations of the world, indeed the estate of matrimony, but not society. By far the most important part of the creation, human society, was only effected when men and women appeared on the stage – of course. And it is this very society that still shows serious shortcomings and that is far from complete. It is man's task to complete this part of the creation in dia-logue with God. And this dialogue occurs especially by means of the Torah, the God-given textbook, and with God as the divine teacher. As the psalmist sings: 'Show me Your ways, o Lord, Teach me Your paths' (Psalm 25:4).

The Torah recognizes many images of God: sometimes he is the Creator, sometimes the Judge, at other times the Saviour or the Law-giver. Perhaps the most important image of God, that always plays a part in the background, sometimes in the foreground, is the image of God as a father educating his children, and in line with it the image of a teacher who educates his people and accompanies it in the learning process of their life. In the oral Torah this image of God as a teacher and an example for man is gone into in all kinds of places. Man is incited to follow God, to 'imitate' him. This is, as said before, the 'imi-tatio Dei', the 'imitation of God'. Some other examples of this 'imita-tion of God' are the following ones.

Abraham is still recuperating after his circumcision in Genesis 18, when 'the Lord appeared to him by the terebinth trees of Mamre, as he was sitting in the tent door in the heat of the day' (Genesis 18,1). The Midrash asks: Why did the Lord appear to Abraham just now, and why did he remain sitting? One of the answers given is that it was the third day after Abraham's circumcision, and that Adonai – praised be He – came to inquire after Abraham's well-being, after his 'shalom'.[16] Of course, God knew how Abraham fared and that was not the reason to call upon him. But God himself shows how to discharge one's duty of visiting the sick. The Midrash connects this scene also with Psalm 18,35, which reads:[17] 'Your condescension has made me great'. What does 'condescension' mean in this respect? It means that God 'condescended', bent to Abraham, allowing him to remain sitting as shown by the text of Genesis 1. This teaches us that the common manners between lord and servant, between one's superior and one's inferior are not valid when one's inferior is ill. Therefore, generally speaking, many Torah rules are suspended for those who are weakened, ill, or old.

Another example about the part the 'imitatio Dei' plays in the process of perfecting society is found in the story of the Tower of Babel. In Genesis 11 we read that the top of this tower should be in the heavens. The text remarks cleverly: 'But the Lord came down to see the city and the tower which the sons of men had built' (v. 5). The oral Torah asks (slightly ironical): why did God come down? Couldn't He watch the tower from heaven? And then the answer: of course He could, but He came down to set an example to all earthly judges to go deeply into a case before passing judgement.[18]

This example of a fair jurisdiction makes me think again about the covenant with Noah I already brought up above for a little while. One of the most important requirements of the Noahide covenant between God and all nations is their pursuit of a just society and a just jurisdiction. A greater part of the Torah is devoted to this end. It is man's task to complete the creation by perfecting human society.

The Road to the world to come.

The road to the perfection of the creation is a road covered by trial and error, a road of learning and practice. I'll deal with it comprehensively in chapter 2. Here I'll mention in short three important aspects of the image of man in Torah, which are significant for the road to the world to come.

In the preceding section we saw how God was depicted in the oral Torah as a Teacher. He's in charge of the heavenly house of learning, in which the Torah is being studied perpetually.[19] The life of someone who lives in the Jewish tradition is, as we will see, a process of learning permanently. Each individual is responsible for and should complete his or her own learning process, even when, preferably, studying together with other people. However, there is no doctrinal authority, there are no popes, synods or faculties of theology, that dictate what should be thought, believed, felt or done. The Rabbi is in the first place an expert one consults if one can't solve a problem. If there is no rabbi available, one should decide oneself, also in difficult questions. In general a Jew is characterized by a strong feeling of subjectivity. But it is a subjectivity that is dialogically embedded in the greater objectivity of the Torah and the Jewish tradition. With the help of Torah and tradition everyone decides for him- or herself how to live, what to do and what to abstain from.

The Jewish-Dutch novelist Abel Hertzberg tells in one of his books the story of the Jew Labi who in a German concentration camp refused to eat soup with horsemeat.[20] His motive was: there is a difference! A difference between clean and unclean. He chose to die rather than defile himself with prohibited food. No one was able to put him off his decision. All others present chose the opposite; they valued life higher than purity. And all were right, because both choices are possible within the objectivity of the Torah and the Jewish Tradition. And yet this Labi shows us the image of man in the Torah more clearly than his fellow prisoners. Someone who lives in accordance with the Torah, should be prepared to accept the consequences of his faith, even when this estranges him from the community. Even when the utmost consequence could be death.

Now another aspect of the image of man in the Torah emerges. Man shouldn't be focussed on, and certainly not exclusively, the effectiveness, the result or the outcome of his actions. More important is the integrity, the authenticity of one's life. If one is going to lose one's authenticity in order to become rich, one should better stay poor. If one is forced to renounce the Torah and God to stay alive, one had better die. Besides, even if someone realizes that acting well in his situation won't be followed by a good result, he should do it yet. In the image of man in Torah lack of effect and result should never be a motive for passivity.

I now reach the last aspect of the image of man in Torah I want to discuss in this chapter: the Torah hardly thinks in terms of result, of productivity. And certainly not in terms of result just for the sake of result, or productivity just for the sake of productivity. Modern images of man, whether capitalistic, Calvinistic, liberal, socialistic or Marxist of colour, take it for granted that man find a greater part of his identity in his work, in his social or economical productivity. The dominating idea in modern western society is that everyone should provide for himself, essentially. Having a job, a highly paid job , is for many people today the highest aim to pursue. Marriage, children, free time, a good diet, peace and quiet, health and a lot more, all is sacrificed easily to function socially and economically.

This attitude, however, is far off from the image of man in the Torah, because labour plays a much less important part in biblical thought.[21] Man, and indeed the entire creation find their identities not during the six workdays, but on the seventh day, the Sabbath, the day of rest, the day without work, without productive labour, the day of the world to come. On that day religious Jews rest and follow once more the example God set them on that very first Sabbath (Genesis 2,1-3). The Creation story was ultimately written with a view to that day of rest and 'shalom', that day of the quality of life. The six workdays with their productive labour simply exist to make the Sabbath possible, not the other way round.

So there is a significant difference between the sabbath and the Christian Sunday. The sabbath is the last day of the week. The week preceding the sabbath, is aimed at the preparation of the next sabbath. The Sunday on the other hand, is the first day of the week and is often seen as preparation of the following week. So the Sunday represents a diametrically opposite vision on work and time than the ideas around the sabbath do: in Judaism the productivity of the workdays serves the sabbatical peace; in Christianity the Sunday serves the productivity of the workdays. Already in antiquity Greek and Roman authors thought the Jews a lazy people because they didn't work every seventh day. But the image of man in the Torah isn't a matter of course, that's just the way it is!

Preview

The image of man in the Torah is as currently today as it was 20 centuries ago. Now that Christianity is losing rapidly its influence on modern culture since the second half of the 20th century, our western society needs new concepts and paradigms urgently. The image of man in Torah not only appeared having resisted the ravages of time, but has yet much to offer to those who take our modern culture seriously. This image presents non-Jews with new ideas and thoughts too, with which modern life can be understood and directed. The image of man in the Torah can help us to find answers to questions that will confront us in the 21st century as well.

For the next chapters I've made a choice from the many aspects that are connected with the image of man in the Torah. Coming up for discussion are: learning, self-reflection and acting socially, in that order. These chapters are followed by a chapter on 'shalom', the advancement of peace and well-being. In the last chapter I'll try to compare the image of man in the Torah with other, prevailing images of man in the world surrounding us. So, one should do as one sees fit.

2 Learn until the World-to-come

In his discourse on the question why the synagogue is popularly called 'shul' (school), the Dutch rabbi S.Ph. de Vries (1870-1944) writes:[22] "The heart of Judaism beats most powerful where one learns. Once a number of Jewish people has settled somewhere, they soon come together to learn. They purchase books, they meet on the sabbath and in the evening, the daily work done, in order to learn. They sit down at a table, guided by someone who feels called to it or who is accepted as a matter-of-course, and they learn. Learn according to the level of knowledge of Jewish matters of those at the table. [...] The learning-room is considered a more important condition for Judaism than the house of prayer. Studying the teachings counterbalances numerous other religious duties. [...] The essence of Judaism is supported by knowledge, by learning Judaism."

Wherever Jews settled for the first time, a place, a room to study in, came first. And indeed very often this place developed into a synagogue, because the study of Torah was regularly interrupted by the daily prayers. So the house of study didn't stem from the synagogue, but the synagogue followed the house of study. And that is the reason why in these parts the synagogue is still called the 'shul' (i.e the Jiddish word for 'school'). This relation between the house of study and the synagogue is very old indeed. The Talmud states that a synagogue may be altered into a house of study, but not the other way round, because that should mean a lessening of intrinsic value.[23] That study and worship are closely connected appears also from the fact that many Jewish scholars – when studying Torah – wear their prayer shawls and phylacteries. Reading (aloud) from the Torah is a central element during the synagogue service as well and the explanation of the pericopes read, became an accepted part between the services.[24]

In this chapter I want to show the importance of learning in Judaism and how this is connected with the image of man in the Torah.

The Torah as a programme of principles

The important place learning occupies in Judaism, originates from the Torah itself. As we saw in the previous chapter, the word 'torah' is derived from a Hebrew verb meaning: 'to indicate, to instruct, to teach or to learn'. So the Torah is a textbook containing instructions for life. That's the reason why Martin Buber (1878-1965) and Franz Rosenzweig (1886-1929) translated the word 'Torah' with the German word 'Weisung'.[25] Contrary to the ideas of those outside Judaism, the Torah doesn't contain detailed prescriptions in general, but mainly principles of justice and on behaviour, formulated in practical terms indeed, but denoting abstract principles.

Already the first word of the Torah makes it clear that the Torah is a program of principles. As we saw in chapter 1, the word 'bêreshit' does not only mean 'in the beginning', but also and the more so 'in principle'. I prefer to translate Genesis 1:1 with: 'In principle God created the heaven and the earth'. In order to be able to apply these principles one should study, investigate and discuss. And this should not only be done by scholars but by everyone who wants to live with the Torah. Studying the Torah is a duty for every Jew. It's about learning first (German: 'lernen') and about teaching (German: 'lehren') only in the second place. For centuries the Jews occupied themselves with this study and the results of all this 'lernen' and 'lehren' were recorded in numerous texts. And in their turn these texts became a source of study: Tanakh (the Hebrew Bible), Mishnah, Talmud, Midrash, etc. And also these texts were provided with comments on comments on comments.

As already seen before, we shouldn't restrict the idea of Torah to the five books of Moses (Genesis – Deuteronomy), 'the Written Torah'. The Torah also includes the extensive oral doctrine of Judaism. This oral Torah mainly consists of (an) interpretation of the written Torah. According to the traditional Jewish view both, the oral and the written Torah, were given to Moses on Mount Sinai. So there is a certain mutual interdependence between both, because the written Tora – and this applies to every law – is based on a meta-system of concepts, rules of law and legal practices which very often aren't mentioned explicitly in it. These concepts, rules of law and legal practices already existed in the oral Torah when the text of the written Torah was recorded.[26] That's why some rabbinic traditions state that Moses in the forty days on Mount Sinai didn't learn the whole Torah, but only the general principles, 'kêlalim' in Hebrew.[27] For the teaching (Hebrew: Torah) of God can't be given in a completed form suitable for all times. With these general principles scholars of all generations would be able to elaborate the details needed at a certain moment. Therefore, statements on Jewish-religious rules of conduct (Hebrew: 'halachah'), take their authority from the way they are based on the Torah. One of these rules of conduct reads, that the scholars decide the 'halachah' by a majority decision.[28]

Connected with this is the notion that the interpretation of the written Torah in Judaism is often more important than the written Torah itself. The written Torah has no meaning without the oral Torah, because it's the interpretation that gives the written Torah its meaning. So important even is the oral Torah that the Talmud states: "Only for the sake of the oral Torah God entered into a covenant [i.e. a cooperation] with Israel".[29] In a way, the written Torah could be called a benchmark, a point of reference in the development of the oral Torah. From the moment the written Torah had been recorded, a benchmark was created that made it possible and obligatory to test new developments in the oral Torah, that is, if they want to be real parts of this oral Torah.

Historically, the final wording of the written Torah in the days of Ezra and Nehemiah coincides with the silence of the prophecy in Israel. The last three prophets were Zechariah, Haggai and Malachi. The part of the prophecy as the revelation of the divine will was taken over by the study of the Torah. According to the subsequent Pharisaic-rabbinic view the direct prophetic revelation had withdrawn from Israel from then on. The divine will could only be discovered and recognized by studying his words from the past.[30] From that moment in time revelation means that scholars with the help of the Torah – that speaks the language of man[31] – are and will be able to define what should and should not be done according to God's will in specific situations.[32]

Consequently, it has become a lot more difficult to appeal to direct revelation. Once God revealed himself directly to Moses on Mount Sinai. Students from later generations tried to understand their teachers again and again to finally be able to understand God. In Judaism direct contact between man and God was and is considered of minor importance than Moses' contact with God on Mount Sinai and his account of that meeting in the Torah. God taught Moses the entire Torah with all its implications in the forty days he spent on Mount Sinai (Exodus 34:28). Consequently, everyone who searches the Torah for answers to his or her questions, won't search it in vain.[33]

What Jews are looking for in the Torah is everything, quite literally. The Torah is not only about certain values or a way of life, nor about wisdom only. The essence of the Torah is: "Delve in it [the Torah] and [continue to] delve in it, for everything is in it."[34] Therefore 'Jewish tradition' and 'Torah' are often interchangeable expressions[35] Besides, everyone will be able to assist the development and renewal of the tradition in his or her own way. The well-known Jewish scholar Chaphets Chayiem (1838-1933) once said to a small boy: "Tell me a bit of Torah". His students asked him: "Whatever can you learn from a small boy?" He answered: "Everyone has his share in the Torah, and this small boy could have an idea not given to me!"[36]

A learning case

A problem that should be overcome when one starts reading and studying the Torah, a problem that occurs in the rest of the Hebrew Bible as well, is the problem of the 'apparent obviousness'. This problem could be demonstrated by means of the rule: "an eye for an eye, a tooth for a tooth" (Exodus 21: 23-25).[a] This passage offers a good example of the misunderstanding that could come up if one doesn't take the Torah as a code of principles of justice but as literal legislation.

---

a   See also: Leviticus 24:17-22.

Many non-Jewish commentators interpreted this rule as "the right to retaliation" (Latin: jus talionis). This interpretation is often accompanied by the idea that the Torah is a cruel and obsolete code of law, by now replaced by Jesus' order to love one another in the gospels.[37] A view like that doesn't do justice to the character of the Torah as a code of principles of justice.[a, 38] So what's the matter here?

The words "an eye for an eye, a tooth for a tooth" are part of a larger text that says in its entirety:

(A) "If men fight, and hurt a woman with child, so that she gives birth prematurely, yet no harm follows, he shall surely be punished accordingly as the woman's husband imposes on him; and he shall pay[b] as the judges determine.
(B) But if any harm follows, then you shall give life for life, eye for eye, tooth for tooth, hand for hand, foot for foot, burn for burn, wound for wound, stripe for stripe" (Exodus 21:22-25).

The text uses the words 'wound' and 'stripe' with a purpose, because these words link up with another, earlier text in the Torah, the appeal to blood feud by Lamech, who exclaims:[c]

"For I have killed a man for wounding me, even a young man for striping me. If Cain shall be avenged sevenfold, then Lamech seventy-sevenfold" (Genesis 4:23-24).

Read against the background of this story about blood feud in Genesis 4, one discovers that the text in Exodus 21 isn't about legalizing retaliation, but rather about the curtailment of the blood feud and blood

---

a   Neither to the gospels as Jewish commentaries to the Torah (see end-note).
b   One could gather from this that another status is attributed to the fetus than is the case in orthodox Christianity.
c   This is an example of a so-called 'gezera shawa', one of the most important exegetic rules in the rabbinic literature. This rule is for example applied when two or more texts within the Torah are linked by means of analogy of words.

revenge, a practice that plays a part of no mean importance in the sense of justice of the people in many cultures until today – and certainly in the Middle East.[a] The above mentioned (B)-quotation from Exodus is the sequel to the (A)-quotation and so this could also imply that the "eye for eye, tooth for tooth"-quotation is not about physical retaliation, but about financial compensation. Consequently, the rabbis conclude that one should read the text as follows: "You shall give the value of an eye for an eye, the value of a tooth for a tooth". Besides one can gather from the end of the (A)-quotation that this isn't about rules for actions of private individuals but for the jurisdiction in court. "Eye for eye, tooth for tooth" doesn't mean "retaliation-in-kind", but practically its opposite, that is, financial compensation imposed by the court of law.[39]

One could imagine that this way of reading the Torah as a consistent declaration of principles leads to other interpretations altogether, than a literal interpretation of miscellaneous texts, that at the same time pays little or no attention to the culture in which the Torah originally functioned. The Torah demands to be studied, to be taught, to be examined, if only because of its character. If one takes the Tanakh, the Hebrew Bible, literally, many statements are even inconsistent with each other. And so one of the very first principles of the rabbinic tradition was that in general the sentences and words of the Tanakh shouldn't be taken literally.[40]

Learning all one's life

In the Jewish tradition learning occupies the central stage. Learning all one's life is the pre-eminent, educational basic principle and it is laid down as such in the various religious codes. The study of the Torah is not only a subject for scholars. From the antiquity onwards it's an issue we would specify today with the term 'adult education'. In the

---

a   The arrival of large numbers of foreigners in the Netherlands even caused the problem of blood feud and blood revenge to become a topical subject again at the beginning of the 21st century.

apocryphal book of Jesus Sirach (ca. 200 BCE) the song of the Wisdom reads: "Draw near to me, ye unlearned, and dwell in the house of learning" (Jesus Sirach 51:23). And a bit further in the song of Wisdom it says: "Let your soul rejoice in my mercy, and be not ashamed of my praise" (id. 51:29). These passages show that the house of learning existed already early on in history in the land of Israel and that it was not a matter of scholars only. A considerable time already before the Common Era the house of learning had achieved a certain authority as a place of study for adults.[a, 41] Yet learning all one's life isn't considered a natural activity in the Jewish tradition, but as something that demands a lot of will power and perseverance. All rules that regulate human life are therefore subordinate to the principle learning all one's life. But here also the idea prevails that what the student learns, should have its effect in his personal life.[42]

In the issue of learning all one's life it's in the first place about the adult who – of his own free will – studies at the level he or she deems fit and he or she is able to deal with. But this self-tuition should take place within the community. One should study preferably together with other people, because "iron sharpens iron" (Proverbs 27:17). The Talmud explains this text from the book of Proverbs as follows:[43] "as one piece of iron sharpens an other [piece], so do two [people], who study Torah together, sharpen each others insights".

In this form of adult education rabbis play an important part as teachers, but they aren't needed at all. One can also learn without the presence of the rabbis. And if any teachers are present they are rather involved as a walking encyclopedia, than as a teacher who actually teaches. Besides, the teachers themselves come to the house of learning to study and, if asked, help others with their study of the Torah. Within this context of students who study independently one should interpret the Talmud's statement:[44] "I have learned much from my teachers, more from my fellow students, but most of my students."

---

a   Scholars, however, disagree about the question to what extent the houses of learning were established and respected institutions in those days (see end-note).

Not everyone needs to reach the same high level. The Torah doesn't demand the same results from everyone, but it does expect that one should give one's all when learning.[45] After all, the greatest scholars never stop learning and should realize that they owe much of their knowledge to others.[46]

Student and Teacher

The knowledge of Torah is not the exclusive right of a hereditary dynasty. Moses wasn't succeeded by his sons[47], because the Torah is the heritage of the Jewish people in its entirety and no Jew is entitled to withhold this heritage from another Jew.[48] Judaism is a religious democracy[49] and the Torah is its constitution. The Torah is the common property of the entire community of Jacob (Hebrew: morasha kêhiloth ja'akov), both men and women. Every Jew and Jewess is considered capable enough to consult the original source of the Torah and to find guidance in it for their daily life. The duty to learn rests on every Jew and therefore the Mishna advises:[50] "Let your house be a meeting place for scholars."

In Jewish dissertations on learning the student's part is at least as important as the teacher's, if not the more so. Thus the Talmud states characteristically that "the world is only maintained by the breath of learning children".[51] This means that the world has only a future thanks to the pupils, not thanks to the teachers. In Judaism man is a student first and only in the second place a teacher.[52] This assumption even means that a teacher who doesn't study anymore, is considered unable to teach well. Compared with the student the teacher's task is two-fold. He is not only expected to teach, but just like the student he is obliged to learn. No man, woman or teacher can leave their student's stage behind and back out of the obligation to learn.

It is said that the rabbis are the only teachers of all religions who consider making their own services redundant, the highest aim of their efforts.[53] As teachers they will try to take their students thus far, that they will be able to examine texts independently. Anyway, this doesn't alter their obligation to teach. After all, it can't be justified morally that a rich man is the only one who profits from his own wealth and neither can it be justified that a scholar is the only one who enjoys his own wisdom. Each Jew, whether he's a teacher or not, is not allowed to withdraw from his obligation to teach the Torah to another Jew, on the condition that he will be able to do so and the other is willing to learn.

Much advice given to teachers in the Talmud, is about how to deal with students. One advice is: "Establish many students",[54] or literally: "Cause many students to stand". We could understand this expression as: "make them stand up, on their own feet, so that they, when they get older, as independent teachers can take care of further passing down the Torah.[55] The real scholar should teach anyone and anywhere he could, and apply his knowledge for the welfare of his fellow-men. He should accept every student who is kind and sincere, and may not test anyone first to discover whether the education will be successful or not.[56] There is an old tradition from the School of Shammai that says: "One should only teach him who's got talent, who's docile, highborn and rich." But the School of Hillel says: "One should teach everyone, because many sinners felt drawn to the study of the Torah, and many righteous, pious and venerable people descended from them."[57] In the Talmud Rabban Gamliel II (end 1st century CE) is reproached with being too critical when he selected his students.[58] When the Talmudic scholars say that one shouldn't teach undeserving students, they only mean people with a bad attitude.[59] After all, one should be willing, eager even to learn. Hillel (end 1st century CE) says: "If there is a generation facing you that loves the Torah, spread your knowledge, but if you are confronted with a generation that has no love for the Torah, gather your knowledge and keep it".[60]

Another piece of advice to the teachers concerns the care with which they should deal with their students and with which to teach them "Pay very much attention to your words and actions as a teacher, because your students may drink them in and die".[61] Who as a teacher says the wrong things or gives the wrong example puts his students on the wrong track with the possible result that he estranges them from the Torah. Besides, teaching the Torah should be done without expecting any gain. The Mishnah says with regard to this issue:[62] "Be not as servants who serve their lord to earn payment". That's the reason why many Torah-scholars were labourers, carpenters, cobblers, charcoal burners, tent-makers etc. etc. Rabbi Jehuda (2nd century CE) used to carry a self-made cask on his shoulder when he entered the house of learning, at least, so the story goes. Then he said, using the cask as a seat for his discourse: "Labour is a grand matter, it honours its master".[63]

Teachers are never allowed to stop teaching, ever. Teaching is compared with sowing and this what Ecclesiastes 11:6 alludes to: "In the morning sow your seed, and in the evening do not withhold your hand". How unwearyingly one should continue to educate students is told in the following tradition about Rabbi Akiva. No one had more students: twenty-four thousand. By the end of his life they'd all lost their lives. They had died of a virulent disease or had perished in the Bar-Kochba-uprising (135 CE). Yet he started again and gathered them around him: Rabbi Meir, Rabbi Jose, Rabbi Yehuda, Rabbi Simeon, Rabbi Nechemya and Rabbi Yochanan the Sandalmaker. They became the "Fathers of Israel".[64]

The teaching-learning process

In this process student and teacher are partners in learning, in teaching and in practice. This partnership defines the way they treat one another. The teacher's affection for his students makes him listen well to them and makes him even guess the questions they don't ask. This relation has its origins in the way God deals with man. God, too, knows man's heart and his questions.

Being a disciple in the sense of a student having a special relation with one specific teacher, plays a minor part in general, because the Jewish education especially intends to enlarge the student's knowledge of the Torah.[65] The teacher doesn't intend to make disciples for himself, but to enhance his students' knowledge. Knowledge transfer does not only occur verbally, but especially by means of actions. In Talmudic days a student did not only commit himself to a rabbi to get acquainted with the Torah, but in particular to learn to act according to the Torah. For example how to deal with food was not only learned by studying the rules, but also by watching how the Torah was embodied in the gestures and acts of the teacher. Living teachers teach the Torah not only by means of words, but also by means of their acts. To realize the full weight and the full meaning of the Torah the student should enter the rabbi's house and watch how he lives according to the Torah. By imitating their teachers, the students learn the acts of the Torah, acts the teachers had learned in their turn from their teachers, and so back to Moses, who learned them by imitating God (imitatio Dei].[66]

The heart, the essence of Jewish education is the personal relation between teacher and student. Consequently, this educational conversation should be a private one, a conversation 'face to face'. In such a conversation the Torah comes to life: the teacher presents the Torah and the student makes himself familiar with the Torah. The teacher invites the student to receive the Torah by studying it. This way, this model of learning doesn't silence the student, but enables him to come to a conversation with his teacher and via the teacher to a dialogue with the Torah.[67] Because it's all about that direct dialogue with the Torah.

Anyway, studying the Torah is not always a matter that passes off smoothly. And although Judaism values peace higher than the truth in general, this doesn't mean that student and teacher won't be allowed to disagree. That's exactly why one learns most from defending one point of view passionately and criticizing another one fiercely. The Talmud comments:[68] 'Even father and son, teacher and student become enemies when [they are] fighting over the meaning of the Torah. But if they don't leave [angrily] until they've become friends again, then the Torah says: waheev bê-supha (Numbers 21:14) i.e. "friendship in [the residence of] supha". However one should not read in this text 'supha' but 'sopha',[a] so that the sentence runs: "friendship at the end".' If only one should leave the house of learning as friends, the fight for the truth may be fought fiercely. Even if one holds the principle that the search for the truth reaches its bounds if peace is in danger, one should only discover where these bounds are by going beyond them now and then. Each living tradition struggles with the dilemma, that the search for the truth and chasing peace can not always be combined and that both are essential for the survival of the tradition.[69]

Laying the foundation

The intensive way of learning, so characteristic for traditional Judaism, asks for a foundation of knowledge and skills that should be build up from childhood. The Torah itself instructs: "And these words which I command you today shall be in your heart. You shall teach them diligently to your children, and shall talk of them when you sit in your house, when you walk by the way, when you lie down, and when you rise up" (Deuteronomy 6:6-7). Learning the Torah is an intensive way of adult education and can only be realized on a broad scale, if children are taught the Torah intensively from childhood by memorizing texts and imitating acts,[b] and at the same time are stimulated to develop their identity as learners by discovering learning and learning through questions. Learning how to ask questions is an important part of the education. "Who's too shy, doesn't learn", so the Mishnah says.[70] Therefore in most Jewish textbooks the material is represented in ask-and-answer form.[71] Even the Talmud begins with a question.[72] If one doesn't teach children the Torah from the very beginning, - so that

---

a   Here the rabbis use the fact that the original Hebrew text of the Torah is written with consonants only. Different vowels could be used to give the words different meanings. By doing so different meanings can appear, that could be important for variant interpretations.

b   One doesn't shrink from such teaching methods, old-fashioned as they may seem in the eyes of many today, because the negative effects are avoided by the combination with discovery learning.

later on they will be able to study it independently -, the houses of learning will become increasingly empty and the Torah will be forgotten.[a]

That's why this Jewish way of learning begins at a very early age and within the family.[b, 73] Officially it ends with the bar- and bat-mitzwah ceremony, when boys of 13 and girls of 12 years old celebrate their religious coming of age. From then on they are considered capable to put that what they have learned into practice.[c, 74] One can't start learning too early. This is derived from the thought that man already starts learning before he's born. The Talmud states that pregnant women tried to influence the foetus by making it listen to the voices of de scholars who were studying the Torah.[75] Each child is supposed to have learned the Torah by heart already in the womb. But once born, an angle touches the child's lips and it forgets everything. Everything should be learned again, this means that in life it's about learning, not about knowing.[76]

Learning at a young age is aimed at habit forming especially. During puberty the child is considered to mature rationally and should learn to reflect on the practices learned. The great rabbinic commentators tried to write their comments that clear, that they could be understood by everyone, scholar or non-scholar alike. Jewish children are taught many stories (aggadah) at a young age already, stories that they will learn to understand when older.[77]

The Talmud says that learning children shouldn't be disturbed, not even for the construction of the temple.[78] Education is considered a condition of existence. A town, in which no one is taught, will perish.

---

a   The main purpose of education should be training young people to take up their own adult education, "learning to learn" as it is called nowadays.
b   Some people consider this idea as essential for a Christian catechesis that wants to learn from the Jewish experience (see endnote).
c   This custom of the bar-mitzwah ceremony affected the early Christians for a long time and it still does so in the Roman Catholic Church even today. In the Reformation Churches it used to be customary to let young people of about 12 be confirmed, as in Geneva in the days of John Calvin (1509-1564) (See endnote).

Even the destruction of Jerusalem is attributed to the fact that one neglected to teach the children. Teachers are even called the guardians of the city.[79] That's the reason why one is allowed to change a synagogue into a house of learning, but not the other way round. Because this is a devaluation in Jewish eyes.[80]

The Jerusalem Talmud reports that at the beginning of the first century CE an important educational innovation took place in Judaism: Simeon ben Shetach, the then leader of the Pharisees, introduced compulsory education for children. Another notice in the Babylonian Talmud tells us however that it has taken quite some time before one gained the correct insight of how the education of children should be organized and of what should be the best age to begin teaching them. Halfway through the first century the Pharisaic Judaism had a well-developed schoolsystem for children from six years old. From that age onwards the children attended the 'beth sefer' (the house of the book). Learning the Hebrew alphabet came first, immediately followed by learning how to read from the first chapter of the book of Leviticus. Once they had mastered this art, they started reading the book of Genesis, followed by the rest of the Torah, the Prophets and the Writings.[a] At ten the children went to the 'Beth Mishneh' (the 'house of repetition').

There they studied the oral Torah, later recorded in the Mishneh, the Talmud and in the Midrash[b]. In those days a thirteen-year-old boy had a ready knowledge of the Hebrew Bible and the oral tradition we can hardly imagine.[81]

The fact that only the written and oral Torah were taught in the schools doesn't mean that the education was more one-sided than our education now. After all, the Torah is not only about religious matters in the narrow sense of the word, but she includes all fields of life. But contrary to our modern educational system, that has broken up into all kinds of different subjects, is the Torah-education an integrated form

---

a   Torah, Prophets and Writings is the Jewish order of the Hebrew Bible. The so-called historical books from Joshua to 2 Kings belong to the Prophets.
b   Several collections of the most important 'midrashim' (plural of midrash).

of education, in which all aspects of a problem come up in mutual coherence. The aim of the primary education in Tanakh and oral Torah was to make thirteen-year-old boys responsible for their own religious and social performance. That period was followed by daily learning in the study-house for those among them who wanted to go on learning Torah.[82]

The methodology of learning

The five following rules of study are sometimes called to be character-istic for the Jewish way of studying:[83]

1. Study all the time,
2. Repeat,
3. Study alone and with other people,
4. Learn by putting it into practice,
5. Plan your own way of studying.

The advice to repeat takes it for granted that there is a certain amount of knowledge that retains its value. Repeating something is done to better remember it. In that case knowledge will be available to solve the questions of the moment. Repetition often causes a better under-standing of matters one didn't understand completely the first time one tried to do so. It's also said that in the long run it's no longer about what you do with it, but what it's doing with you.[84]

The main learning aim of childhood is to learn how to memorize texts, how to store this material into one's memory. In this respect the Talmud speaks a plain language:[85] "Do not accept pupils under the age of six. Once six, cram them as full as an ox." This is a metaphor with a hidden, witty meaning, because 'as an ox' (in Hebrew 'kêtorah') is a pun on the word 'Torah'. The pupils' memories were trained to such a degree that all sorts of parts of the texts could even be recited in the back to front order. They read and rehearsed the texts aloud in order to make themselves familiar with them. One assumed that someone who'd studied silently, just because of this, would lose the gathered knowledge after three years. Memorizing came first and only then one's own understanding and thinking for oneself came up.[86]

Studying together is important because this can help to correct mistakes, to reinforce motivation and to gain more in-depth knowledge.[87] Students who learn collectively play the part of student and teacher in turns, and so does the teacher himself. If teachers no longer should learn from their own teaching, their profession shouldn't be so well thought-of in the Jewish tradition as is the case now and God should never be represented as a teacher.[a] By teaching one takes one of the courses that can lead us to the knowledge of the Torah. The rabbis have always been aware of this aspect, witness Rabbi Chanina's saying (early 3rd century CE), already quoted before:[88] "I learned a lot from my teachers, more yet from my colleagues, but most from my students." Learning surpasses teaching.[89]

The value of learning together is expressed in every conceivable way. One tradition reads as follows:[90] "When ten people are together and study the Torah, the divine presence (shêchinah) will rest upon them." But the same is said about someone who studies alone: "And what teaches us that this is even so for one person [who studies the Torah on his own]? Because it is said: In every place where I record My name I will come to you [singular], and I will bless you [singular] (Exodus 20:24b)." The combination of learning individually and collectively forms the basis for the learning process. Learning together with someone else has been done in Judaism for centuries:[91] "Provide yourself with a teacher, a friend to study with and judge everyone according to his best side".

Learning and teaching, two essentially different processes, are approached methodically in Judaism. Not only the individual should plan his own learning process alone ánd together with other people, but also the community should make learning possible. One should make a real effort to found and maintain schools and houses of learning. Adults should devote themselves more to learning than to being taught. This process of adult education and learning all one's life

---

a   See the last paragraph of this chapter.

should happen and happens especially in the houses of learning. Therefore, teaching methods have been developed in the Jewish tradition especially for adults, methods in which the students are stimulated to learn ànd teach themselves.[92]

Learning Torah and daily life

We already saw that in the days of the Talmud the teaching of the Torah had to be done free of charge. That's the reason why many rabbis practised a profession or trade that prevented them from studying all day long. This combination of studying and practising their daily work however, has not been a matter of course for each scholar. The Talmud contains an interesting discussion on this issue, a discussion that tries to fathom two scriptural passages.[93] The first text concerns daily life: "... then I will give you the rain for your land in its season, the early rain and the latter rain, that you may gather in your grain, your new wine, and your oil" (Deuteronomy 11:14). The second text is about the study of Torah and says: "This Book of the Law shall not depart from your mouth, but you shall meditate in it day and night," (Joshua 1:8). There is an apparent, internal contradiction in these two texts, because one can't simply gather in the crops and study the Torah at the same time.

In the discussion that arose about this problem, two views confronted each other. Rabbi Jishma'el (2e century CE) reached the first solution: "Suppose I had thought that this last verse [Joshua 1:8] is meant to be taken literally, so to prevent this the verse in Deuteronomy has been written. Thus it is pointed out to me that, next to the study of the Torah, I am obliged to practise an earthly trade as well." His contemporary Rabbi Simeon bar Jochai on the other hand, solves the apparent contradiction between both verses quite differently by adding a third bible-verse. He wonders: "It can't be Deuteronomy's intention that man ploughs in the days of ploughing, sows in the days of sowing, harvests in the days of harvesting, threshes in the days of threshing and winnows in the days of winnowing? After all, what would be the result of the higher calling to study the Torah? Both verses [in Deuteronomy and in Joshua] should allude to different situations. When one wants to observe the will of God completely, one should have others do the earthly work, as is written in Isaiah 61:5: "Strangers shall stand and feed your flocks". However, when one doesn't fulfill the will of God and neglects the study of Torah, one should do one's work oneself as is written [in Deuteronomy]: That you may gather in your grain, your new wine, and your oil".

About a century later Rabbi Abaji (320-376 CE) commented on both points of view. He observes: "Many did as Rabbi Jishma'el had advised and managed to properly fulfill both obligations – working for their daily bread and studying the Torah. Those who tried to live in accordance with Rabbi Simeon bar Jochai's ideal didn't succeed usually". This is the Talmud's realistic point of view: one should not only study the Torah, but also take care of the material welfare of the community.

The relation between learning and doing

In addition to the fact that the study of Torah and everyday life should be combined, the relation between learning and putting this into practice is also an important issue in the rabbinic literature. And indeed, there are a lot of stories and sayings about this relationship between learning and doing. The Talmud for instance, cites the words of Simeon the Just (3rd century BCE):[94] "The world stands on three things: on [learning] the Torah, on the service [of God], and upon acts of loving-kindness." There is an organic coherence between the three acts mentioned: learning the Torah causes man to serve God and to deal with his fellow man humanely. The Jewish point of view is: the society can't exist without those three activities. Advancing humanity – one could even say: checking man's inclination to depravity – is one of the most important purposes of the Therefore it's most important that the study of the Torah not only leads to knowledge but also to acts. The Talmud tells us about a discussion between some rabbis in the days of the emperor Hadrian[a] (76-138 CE), who'd forbidden the study in the houses of learning. It says:[95] "It so happened that Rabbi Tarphon and the leaders reclined in the upstairsroom of the house of Nitsa in Lod (i.e. Lydda). And they asked themselves: What is more important, studying or acting, learning or doing? Rabbi Tarphon began to speak and said: Doing is more important. Rabbi Akiva answered and said: Learning is more important. Then all the other people said: Learning is more important because learning leads to doing (the right things)". So this story tells us that even in a time when learning is forbidden, one should go on learning, because otherwise the right conduct will be lost.Torah.

Another saying about the relation between learning and doing in the name of Hillel (1st century BCE) goes:[96] 'An untaught man (ignoramus) can't be a chassid'. A 'chassid' is someone who consciously tries to live according to God's intentions and therefore approaches his fellow men amicably. What Hillel means is that one needs at least some knowledge of the Torah to be able to associate with one's neighbour in a correct way. No other rule of conduct in the Torah is more important than the encouragement to learn. The study of the Torah is even considered to be more important than all other commandments,[97] because this study should be followed by practical actions.[98] That's why studying ànd doing the Torah is often called a way of life. Empty, pompous notions that can't be realized in human life are certainly not Torah-notions.[99] So much theology and philosophy lose their value. One of the basic rules in Judaism is that what one does is more important than what one thinks. One even has to do better than the fixed rules, the 'halachah', prescribe. After all, the halachah is directed at the average human being and is only laid down by the rabbis when the majority of the people will be able to keep it.[100] Besides, each man is expected to do more – within the limits of one's own possibilities – and to live more piously than the halachah prescribes.

_____

a   The one of the Wall and of the so-called first Holocaust (136 CE).

Learning is indeed a preparation to doing, directed at improving one's conduct and maintaining society. This process only stops when one dies,[101] one learns until the world-to-come.

Learning and the image of man in the Torah

The most important reason why learning is so important in the Jewish tradition lies in the Jewish-biblical image of man, or, in other words, in the ideas about man in his relation toward God. This relation is brought up in the first chapters of Genesis. The rabbis do not read these stories in the first place as an account of historical events from a dim and distant past, but as an introduction to the Torah: if we want to know which part the Torah should play in the life of man, we should have an image of man.

In Genesis 1 two elements are of importance. In the first place man has been created as a physical being in line with the entire material creation and on the same day as the animals. In the second place man has been created in God's image and likeness. So man's position in the creation is between the animals and God. Contrary to the animals, created 'each according to its kind' and so unable to change their being animals, man has been created 'in the image of God'. And, in Genesis 1, this God exactly creates and creates. Just like the animals man is bound to the material reality of which he is a part, but as the image of God and within that material reality man is a creating being as well: he is God's partner in his creation.[a]

Now the question could be asked what is left for man to create, considering the fact that God has already created everything and 'saw that it was good (tov)'. The expression 'and God saw that it was tov', however, is used in Genesis 1 for all living beings immediately after their creation, except for man. The conclusion is obvious: all living beings have been created to perfection, except man. Man just should

---

a   Hardly any clues are to be found in the Bible and in the ancient rabbinical Judaism for the idea that man is only expected to reach his final destination after his death.

become 'tov', i.e. completed. In this process he himself could play an important part, being a partner in the creative process, because in that quality he is responsible for the perfection of his own human existence. Read in this way the first chapter of Genesis is not an account of historical events but an philosophical program of principles.

Therefore, the duality of the material and the divine is characteristic for human life. On the one hand man has been made of dust of the ground, on the other God has blown the breath of life into his nostrils (Genesis 2:7b). This being 'from here' as well as 'from above' isn't considered in ancient Judaism as an ontological distinction between body and soul, but as an ethical distinction between the two motives present in man: the inclination to do evil (jetsèr ha-ra) and the inclination to do well (jetsèr ha-tov). As both inclinations were created by God, the evil inclination is not only bad. Now it is man's task to use the evil inclination for the better, as I already stated in chapter 1. In the Jewish tradition the belief can be found that even without the evil inclination physical and cultural survival won't be possible. That's the reason why it shouldn't be stamped out or suppressed. The evil inclination is sometimes called the leaven in the dough:[102] a wrong dose spoils the dough, but without it it's tasteless. In order to find out how to use the evil inclination for the better, one studies the Torah. The fight against the evil inclination lasts one's whole life and so one should study one's whole life and one should test in practice what one has learned one's whole life.[103] Concerning this Hillel says:[104] 'Don't trust yourself until the day of your death'. That is: Don't you ever think that you have finally overcome the evil inclination.

The fact that man is God's partner in the process of creation puts responsibility on God as well as on man. In Genesis 2 and 3 this thought is further elaborated from the knowledge that the relation between God and man isn't a static fact but a dynamic process in which man fulfils its part as co-creator with ups and downs. After all, man as co-creator isn't a servile creature. Characteristic for both his inclinations is that he has free choice: he's able to create, but also to destroy; he's able to do well but also to do evil. That's why only man is given tasks to perform. No other creature is free to choose between doing something and not doing something (cf. Deuteronomy 11:16-17; 30:19). Man can honour God's assignments, but can also ignore them. In the Talmud a saying of Rabbi Chanina is handed down that puts the dynamics between God's omnipotence and man's freedom tersely into words:[105] "All things are in the hands of the Eternal, except the awe for the Eternal". The image of man in the Torah is based on the dynamic relation between the freedom of choice on the one hand and his responsibility towards God on the other. Everyman should learn to live with that tension between freedom and responsibility. Responsibility defines freedom, freedom defines responsibility.

Now it's important to get to know what – in these dynamics between freedom and responsibility - the awe for the Eternal asks from man, so we should try and gain insight into and define the notions of creating and destroying, of good and evil. Studying Torah could be of great help. The Torah supplies us with instructions and definitions, directions and obligations by means of assignments often linked with positive and negative prospects ("promises") about the consequences of human actions. The part the Torah-assignments play with regard to human freedom, is explained in a rabbinic commentary on Exodus 32:16. It is pointed out that this text from the Torah could be read in two ways. At first sight this text about the two tables with the ten assignments, the ten commandments reads: "Now the tablets were the work of God, and the writing was the writing of God engraved on the tablets." But then the rabbinic commentator remarks: "Don't read 'engraved' (charut), but read 'freedom' (chèrut), and the sentence reads: "On the tablets: freedom", because anyone who studies the Torah is a free man.[106] The point is that the assignments of the Torah do not only restrict human freedom, but also give a lot of freedom! It's true, the ten commandments or the ten words (Exodus 20) impose restrictions on man, but as a matter of fact they're meant to protect the religion and the freedom of one's fellow man. If man is robbed from his freedom, e.g. by injustice, violence or suppression, he no longer will be able to comply with his being God's image.[107] Therefore, it's the assignments (Hebrew: mitzwot)[a] and the promises of the Torah that will help us realize our responsibility as co-creators. The Torah often combines them. In that case the 'mitzwoth' are being formulated in de form of an assignment with a prospect: "Honor your father and your mother, that your days may be long upon the land which the LORD your God is giving you" (Exodus 20:12), because then your children will honor you when you've grown old.

The paradise-story on the original sin deals especially with the essential question which part these assignments of God play in the process of perfection of man. The gist of the story is, that if and when man doesn't study seriously God's directions and doesn't follow them, this leads to an attitude in life that causes his downfall: he will be expelled from paradise. From Eve's words in Genesis 3:3 the rabbis derive that Adam and Eve hadn't studied the assignment God had set them properly. That's why the serpent could easily move Eve to do the wrong thing. But the end of the story makes it clear as well that the paradise is only closed at one side and could still be reached in the roundabout way of the Torah, the way of assignments and promises.

From the above we could conclude that learning plays an important part in fulfilling God's assignment to be his image. Contrary to the Socratic image of man, in which insight obtained by learning leads automatically to acting well, is this not the case in the Jewish tradition.[108] It should indeed lead to it, but the rabbis know only too well that someone who observes the rules precisely, can – for all that – behave like a villain, as could be the case for instance with all those economical activities not mentioned specifically in the Torah. For instance: what about asking exorbitant prices in times of shortage? What about ruthless competition that leads to someone's bankruptcy? What about using foreknowledge in the stockmarket to enrich oneself? Does one really inform the customer about quality deficiences? And

---

a   The Hebrew word 'mitzwot', usually translated with 'commandments' and sometimes understood as strict rules, should be better rendered with 'tasks' or 'assignments' man should fulfil with the help of his own knowledge and insight.

what about financing an ill-fated company to get a grip on the borrower as a debtor? The reverse can also happen: someone who knows only a little about the Torah, can really walk in 'the way of the earth', the 'dèrech èrets', in other words, behave socially-minded.

The only way to reconcile theory and practice is to study the application of the Torah again in the light of the Torah. Even someone who applies the rules of the Torah from false motives can acquire good behaviour and pure motives – in the long run, that is. The Torah is not only a doctrine but also a way of life. The study of the Torah is both a study of the doctrine and a study of life. And one should be prepared to recognize the fact that mistakes could be made. That's what the Torah means with the fear of the Lord. One's own wrong behaviour or that of other people should be studied to obtain self-improvement.[109] In the Jewish tradition all learning aims, one could set oneself, are subordinate to one learning aim only: one doesn't study in order to be able to practise a profession, not even that of a rabbi, let alone to obtain power and authority, but to improve oneself and one's behaviour – and in doing so to improve society. One learns with the object of becoming 'whole'. And a 'whole' man is, according to the image of man in the Torah, someone who knows the Torah, fears God, fulfils his assignments, makes himself familiar with these and is prepared – if there are no other options left – to sacrifice his life for the sanctification of the name of God.[110] The perfection of life is something that could and should be learned. Man, as God's partner, is able to do superhuman things, as an individual and together with others.[111]

God as the heavenly teacher

From the above we could gather that in the Torah and in Judaism man is – in principle – a learning being in his relation to God. In line with this God is seen as the heavenly Teacher. In the first chapter I already mentioned some examples of the 'imitatio Dei', such as the story of the tower of Babel (Genesis 11). This story tells that God 'descended' to have a good look at the tower the people wanted to build, a tower 'whose top (is) in the heavens'. The question whether the Holy One, praised be He, couldn't have watched this from the heavens, is answered with the observation that He, in doing so, teaches the earthly judges to examine every case thoroughly before passing judgement.[112] In many other texts as well, God's actions are explained as models of learning for man.

The rabbinical literature hardly concerns itself with the question what – spoken philosophically – could be meant with 'the image of God' in which man has been created. One doesn't understand this as philosophy but as an assignment, and especially an assignment for man to develop his abilities in such a way that human existence will be raised to a higher level of life. This assignment is indicated with the term 'making holy': 'Consecrate yourselves therefore, and be holy, for I am the LORD your God. 8 (Leviticus 11:14; 19:2; 20:7, 26). The Talmud explains:[113] 'As He clothes the naked (Genesis 3:21), you should clothe the naked. As He visits the sick (Genesis 18:1), you should visit the sick. As He buries the dead (Deuteronomy 34:6), you should bury the dead. As He comforts the mourners (Genesis 25:11), you should comfort the mourners'. In the Eighteen Benedictions (Shemoneh Esreh one of the most important prayers of Judaism is said about God that He 'supports the falling, heals the sick and sets free' the chained. These benefactions are also explained as examples for man.[114]

Judaism sees God as its heavenly teacher and this image distinguishes it from many other religions. Contrary to idolatry which considers material forms as essential to come into contact with the gods, the Torah says that during the learning process in which the student searches for clues how to do God's will, he will meet the Lord God, praised be He. "With whom is God?" asks the Talmud. The answer says: "With him who studies [the Torah]".[115] There is no mediator, who must be worshipped, between God and man, but a learning process.[116]

3 Prayer, a Bridge between Earth and Heaven

In all nations religion and prayer have always been closely connected. Songs of praise, asking or begging, and thanksgiving are the three ingredients that occur in all manners of prayer. However, depending on one's ideas about the relation between man and the divine, prayer can have another function and quite other accents can be laid in prayers. For example the Greeks and Romans prayed at all occasions: at mock fights and spectacles, at the opening of public and council meetings, at elections of magistrates, at the beginning of a war or a battle, even at the hunt and at entertainment.[117] Next to praising the gods such prayers were often characterized by questions or pleas to a more powerful being, who grant or refuse as he or she pleased. The Roman prayer regularly asks for the favour of the Gods: "Let Thou be favoured". After they were heard, prayers can also express eternal gratitude.[118]

In Christianity this tripartition "praise, asking or pleading, and thanksgiving" also occurs.[119] Although the idea about the divine in Christianity differs strongly from the one in the polytheistic paganism, we often find in Christian prayer a strong tendency to asking and begging as well. Phrases like "Lord, have mercy upon us" are repeated frequently and particularly in the so-called intercessory prayers God's help is invoked with regards to all sorts of daily needs. The Calvinistic scholar Ursinus (1534-1583), one of the compilers of the Heidelberg Catechism, described the essence of prayer for example as follows:[120] "Invocation of the true God, …. in true conversion of the heart …, in which conversion one beseeches the needs, physical or spiritual, from God, or after having received them, thanks Him". The very word 'beseech' very much emphasizes the questions and pleas for help and favours. And although praise has formed an important part of the Christian Liturgy for ages on end – and certainly so in the monastic tradition[121] –, that doesn't alter the fact that 'praying' in our society under the influence of the more popular Christianity is especially seen as a way to win God over to oneself, to get things done from Him, or to inform Him about one's personal needs. In this chapter I will show that Jews, under the influence of the Torah, pray in a different way from Christians, generally speaking.[122]

Jewish ideas about prayer

The name for 'prayer' that happens most in Hebrew is *têfillah*. Contrary to the word 'prayer', the word *têfillah* doesn't refer to praying, asking, pleading in the first place. At a first introduction already with the Jewish way of prayer it is obvious that 'asking in the restricted sense' only constitutes a limited part of the daily prayers.[123] The word *têfillah* is derived from a Hebrew verb-stem that means 'to judge'. The cognate word *hitpalel*, often translated with 'to pray', is a reflexive form of that verb. The true meaning is 'to judge oneself (before God)', 'to make oneself judge and investigator', 'to seek and ask for justice'.[124] So when someone is praying, he/she judges him/herself "before God", because if someone wants to be able to judge, one needs a criterion. In the Greek Delphi the main adage was: 'Know Thyself', the maxim in Jewish prayers is however: 'When you pray, know before Whom you stand'.[125] This self-assessment before God is done three times a day with the help of the 'Siddur', the prayer book, that is filled with texts collected and arranged over the centuries.

So, in the first place prayer is in Judaism a form of self-reflection. During prayer man frees himself from the drag of daily life. Then he's concentrated on his task in life, his responsibility and on the question of what God wishes him to do. Prayer or *têfillah* is having a conversation with God by reciting the texts from the tradition. Via these words God speaks to man, who listens to those words.

In this way, prayer points out to us time and again, that there is a higher aim in life than expanding our our property and pleasure. Têfillah wants man to realize constantly that he lives in God's world. So when praying man opposes actively the idea that he is only a biological, animal being, driven by instincts and passions. By means of prayers, Judaism constantly points out the special character of man and his psyche. The Jewish doctrine confronts us with man's personality, his feeling for things spiritual and ethical with its possibilities of sanctifying one's life. In the Jewish prayer man's outlook on life comes first and may then be followed by prayer in the sense of 'asking' and 'begging'. Psalm 19 contains the essence of the Jewish prayer in a nutshell:[126]

a) a contemplation on nature as God's creation (verses 1-7);
b) a contemplation on our ethical principles as given in the Torah (verses 8-12);
c) the consequences for our way of life and the prayer for support so that we don't fail in our duties (verses 13-15).

Psychologically the origin of prayer is found in man's desire for communication with the divine presence. Man searches for the possibility to open his heart and spirit to the divine. The roots of this desire are found in the feeling of imperfection, especially in times of stress, and in the desire to free oneself from the limitation of sin and from the bondage of evil. At a higher level prayer originates from the search for the archetypical ideal that directs man to the source of goodness and final perfection. Besides, prayer can also stem from the feeling of astonishment about God's tremendous creation and the wonders that every day show His goodness and love like the wonder of the human body and its normal functions. In line with this is prayer also an answer of gratitude for the good gifts of God in life, for one's living, food, health and happiness, for the power to overcome adversity and to recover from illness. There is gratitude for sunny weather and rain in their season, for children and grandchildren, for hope in the future and for the expectation of liberation.

The Jewish prayer doesn't deny the fact that there is much need and sorrow in the world, but it doesn't allow it to paralyze itself. After all, as we've seen already in the previous chapters, someone who's praying is seen as God's co-creator in the creation. Prayer is an important instrument to fulfil that task as a co-worker. That's why the

Jewish prayer concentrates on the good things in this world so that man realizes what God wants in and with the world. So prayer bridges earth and heaven.[127]

However, a theological motive for prayer can be put forward: God longs for the prayers of man.[128] The medieval Jewish scholar Maimonides (1135-1204) explains that it is a mitswah, a holy task, to pray every day, because:[129] 'It is said: "You shall serve the Lord your God" (Exodus 23:25). From the tradition we know that this serve means pray, because it is said: "And you shall serve Him with all your heart" (Deuteronomy 11:13). The [ancient Jewish] sages say: "What is serve Him with all your heart? It's prayer"'.

We also see that essentially a prayer is not a question, but an answer to God's desire that man occupies himself with Him. Yet there is another reason why praying can't be understood as asking solely. The words of a prayer are not only directed to God but also to oneself. What is asked from God or said about Him is at the same time a task for oneself.[130] If, for instance, in the prayer of thanksgiving after the meal one says about God that he feeds all and everyone because his love knows no bounds, then, at the same time, this can be considered an assignment for the one who is praying, to feed one's neighbour, if he needs to be fed. That is the *imitatio Dei*, the imitation of God, we already met as an important aspect of the image of man in the Torah. A quite radical say even reads, that God doesn't need our prayers, but he needs us, because he made us partners in his creation. Prayers are meant to keep the notion of our assignments alive, that God waits for us.[131]

The contents of the prayers

In the previous chapter we saw that primarily a prayer isn't an appeal to God. It's neither about praising God in the first place. Prayer is sometimes defined as quoting – in God's presence, that is – a carefully written anthology of biblical and post-biblical texts, especially collected to that end in the book of prayer.[132] In this section I'll give a concise summary of the contents of the prayers.

The Jewish book of prayer, the *Siddur*, consists for a large part of biblical texts and texts from the Talmud. Over the centuries many prayers were added as well. All these texts were put in a certain order, apparently without any plan. Yet one feels intuitively there must be a reason for the insertion of the prayers and their fixed order.[133] The Siddur – the word means 'order'- contains all prayers for private and public use, for weekdays, sabbath days and holidays. The Siddur is the final product of a long process that lasted many centuries. During these centuries theological insights, cultural preferences and historical experiences left their traces in the texts. As the Bible and the Talmud were rounded off and could only be supplemented with commentaries, glosses and notes in the margin, the Siddur however remained always open to change and addition from new situations and needs. For example, because of the life-threatening situations in the diaspora (*galuth*) many prayers came into being, which are still being said especially in the morning prayers on Mondays and on Tuesdays.[134]

The Siddur includes the daily routine of prayers, the year cycle and the way from the cradle to the grave. Everything can be found in the Siddur: from eating and drinking to national remembrances and messianic expectations. The Siddur is considered almost as holy as the Bible. The Bible is seen as the account of God's revelation to Israel, the Siddur is the account of Israel's self-revelation to God. Scholars study the Bible and the Talmud, the people read the Siddur. The Siddur connects with the words once spoken by the ancestors and that will once be spoken by the children.[135]

Without diminishing the importance of the other prayers in the Siddur there are two prayers which can easily be regarded as the most important ones, because in a sense they are the centre around which the service of prayer has been built since biblical times. The first one is the so-called Standing-prayer (*Amidah*) and the second one is the Hear-Israel-prayer (*Shêmah-Yisrael*). Another name for the Standing-prayer is the 'Prayer of the eightteen benedictions' (*Shêmoneh Esrei*), because it used to consist of eightteen stanzas, now nineteen. This prayer is the core of the Jewish liturgy. Each stanza ends with a benediction. We get an impression of this prayer when we list these benedictions:[136]

1. Blessed are You, Lord our God, Protector of Abraham.
2. Blessed are You, Lord our God, who revives the dead.
3. Blessed are You, Lord our God, the holy God.
4. Blessed are You, Lord our God, giver of knowledge.
5. Blessed are You, Lord our God, who desires repentance.
6. Blessed are You, Lord our God, gracious One who forgives abundantly.
7. Blessed are You, Lord our God, Redeemer of Israel.
8. Blessed are You, Lord our God, who heals the sick of His people Israel.
9. Blessed are You, Lord our God, who blesses the years.
10. Blessed are You, Lord our God, who gathers together the dispersed of His people Israel.
11. Blessed are You, Lord our God,who loves righteousness and judgement.
12. Blessed are You, Lord our God, who breaks the power of his enemies and subdues the malicious.
13. Blessed are You, Lord our God, the support and security of the righteous.
14. Blessed are You, Lord our God, builder of Jerusalem.
15. Blessed are You, Lord our God, who makes the glory of deliverance to flourish.
16. Blessed are You, Lord our God, who hears prayers and supplications.
17. Blessed are You, Lord our God, who restores His Divine Presence to Zion.
18. Blessed are You, Lord our God, whose name is goodness, it is pleasing to give thanks to Thee.
19. Blessed are You, Lord our God, who blesses His people with peace.

This Standing-prayer is prayed three times a day: during the morning-, afternoon- and evening-prayer. By concentrating on the text of this prayer, that dwells on the needs of every day, but also places these needs in a rich religuous and historical context, the outlook of the one who prays, is widened. The Standing-prayer diverts the attention from the own egoistic ego to the communities one is a part of: the local community, the people, the human race. The text of this prayer also leads from the present to the history, to the origin of God's people, to the future and to the final destination, to the days of the messiah and the ultimate peace of the world.[137]

The second important prayer text is the Hear-Israel-prayer. It's part of the morning- and evening-prayer. It's in fact a collection of three texts from the Torah: Deuteronomy 6:4-9, Deuteronomy 11:13-21 and Numbers 15:37-41. The first verse: 'Hear o Israel, the Lord is our God, the Lord is one', is often called the only Jewish Creed. It expresses the basic idea of God's unity, who is both 'the ETERNAL' (*Adonai*), de God of Love, as well as 'our God' (*Eloheinu*), de God of Justice.[138] In early rabbinical terms reciting the Hear-Israel-prayer is called 'accepting the kingship of heaven'. This prayer belongs to the oldest Jewish prayers being recited daily.[139] And so this prayer is proof of the fact that the Jewish concept of prayer as self-reflection reaches back far beyond the beginning of the Common Era, for if there is one prayer that doesn't consist of begging and asking, not even of praising and giving thanks, it should be this Hear-Israel-prayer. Indeed, this prayer is introduced by two blessings and ended by a third which deal with the same themes as Psalm 19.[a]

In the Jewish prayer praise and thanksgiving (*bêrachah*, plural *bêra-choth*) takes an important place. However, no absolute distinction can be made between praise and giving thanks.[140] Many prayers in the synagogue are expressions of gratitude for God's many good gifts. It starts already when one gets up with the first morning-prayer in which God is praised for the new day. The Jewish liturgy knows blessings that go specifically with a number of experiences. Who, for instance, goes into the countryside in spring and suddenly sees flowering trees, says:[141] 'Blessed are You, Lord our God, king of the universe,

---

a   See above.

who hast made your world lacking in nought, but hast produced therein goodly creatures and goodly trees wherewith to give delight unto the children of men."[a] The rabbis teach us that one should thank God for good and evil.[142] Only when the messiah will have come all prayers will stop, but for praise and thanksgiving. Praise however is not a means to please God. It's rather a means to express gratitude for the everyday marvels of life. Pious people feel the urge to praise God, but are at the same time aware of the inadequacy of words. The rabbis warn for excessive praise, which in fact belittles God's greatness.[143]

Hebrew knows several verbs for praise. The verb *bareich* [the noun *bêrachah* is a derivative], means in the first instance 'to bow the knee', next also 'to bless and/or to praise'. Praising, man blesses God in stead of man being blessed by God. Blessing is a kind of honouring God. The above printed praises of the Amidah or Standing-prayer show a clear sense of being dependend on God.[144]

The command (*mitswah*) to bless God is mentioned in Deuteronomy 8:10 for the first time. This text is the starting point for 'Grace after meals'. Praise is in the relation with God no one-way communication, but mutual.[145] God makes us enjoy His creation and we praise Him. This means that praise can only be said in a situation as worded in that praise. For example, the blessing over bread runs as follows: "Blessed are You, Lord, our God, master of the universe, who brings forth bread from the earth". It may only be said when actually bread is eaten. This is altogether true for the opposite: the bread may only be eaten after the blessing. This blessing "Blessed are You, Lord, our God" is not meant to be recited indiscriminately. Even the blessing over the rainbow for example can only be said when actually seeing a rainbow. If one doesn't keep to it, such a blessing is considered a useless blessing, even if the intentions are good. Worse, it's a matter of taking God's name in vain as meant in Exodus 20:7.[146]

A certain sense for the wonders of every day is the source for the blessings. The order of daily life is certainly not meant to make us indifferent to the very fact that there is an order.[147] We take many

---

a   Hertz, Daily Prayer Book, 1976.

things around us for granted. Judaism however, wants us to experience all these matters consciously and see them as daily gifts from God. This too is the meaning of the blessings preceding the Hear-Israel-prayer, that bless God because of His creation and His Torah: it is God who every day, as it were, creates the world time and again, and presents us with the Torah. All that is old and familiar and all we are used to and not inclined to pay extra attention to, of all this Judaism wants us to appreciate it anew and to experience it as a gift from God.[148]

Finally, some other remarks in the wording of the blessings. Blessings are never in abstract wordings. Just like a meeting with God won't take place in transcendency, but in the here and now, in the real reality, so the blessing has a specific content.[149] The wording however, presents us with a grammatical problem:

a. the first part of the blessing is in the second person singular: "Bessed are **You**, Lord";
b. next the first person plural: "**our** God, Master of the Universe";
c. and finally the sentence shifts to the third person singular: "**who** brings forth bread from the earth".

Though grammatically strange, this wording is precisely characteristic for the polarity of nearness (1st and 2nd person) and distance (3rd person), not of fear, but of lofe and veneration, of immanence and transendence, so characteristic of the Jewish-religious experience.[150]

The language of the prayers

Praying can be done in every language. Yet the text of the Jewish Book of Prayers is in Hebrew. The Talmud teaches us that there are four languages: Latin, best to conduct war in, Greek best to use for singing, Persian best for complaining and Hebrew best for praying.[151] Some rabbis even opposed against prayer in Aramaic, a sister-language of

Hebrew, but prayers in other languages than Hebrew were never ruled out entirely.[152] Even the Hear-Israel-prayer and the Standing-prayer may be said in each and every language.[153] However, Hebrew is preferable, because it knows nuance and expresses feelings no other language can raise in the same way. That's for instance the case with the feeling of Israel's unity everywhere and through all ages. The use of Hebrew as the language of prayer has greatly stimulated this unity through all ages and prevented, sometimes in spite of great internal differences, the desintegration of Judaism.[154]

That doesn't alter the fact that a lot of Jews have problems under-standing Hebrew texts, which is not always experienced as negative though. For it's more important in a prayer service to say the words of the prayer together as an act of piety, than to tell God something He doesn't know yet. Some people characterize the prayer in the first place as an emotional-aesthetic experience instead of a rational-intellectual activity. That's the reason why the meaning of the words of a prayer are not always that important. It's more about the percep-tion one experiences during the prayer. It's a bit like watching the sun set, when one isn't so much inclined to ask for its meaning. Praying isn't after all 'talking to God', but an emotional reflection on one's own place in life.[155] In such a view on prayer the use of Hebrew as the lan-guage of prayer needn't be an unsurmountable problem as long as the one who prays is willing to study that language a little. It is certainly not necessary to understand every verse and every word of the prayer to feel involved with the emotional overtones of the prayers. Many prayers are passed down in traditional melodies. And according to some simple silence is even the highest form worship.[156]

Spontaneous and set prayers

Below I'd like to pass in review some various aspects of the Jewish prayer praxis. The first aspect concerns the opposition between spon-taneous and set prayers. A spontaneous prayer is often called 'a prayer of expression' (expression of the feeling of that particular moment) and a set prayer is often called 'a prayer of empathy' (empathizing the words of the tradition).[157] In the Jewish prayer praxis the last form, the established or set prayer, happens most. A correct mood isn't required. By reading the words, saying them and sensing them, their meaning will get through to us. Words first, feelings next. A set prayer-text confronts us with positive thoughts and considerations we can't think up ourselves or can formulate less well.[158]

Yet spontaneity has always been considered very important. When Rabban Gamliel II (ca 100 CE) canonized the early synagogue prayers, some of his contemporaries disagreed, because they were afraid that the prayers would lose their spontaneity.[159] However, the majority of the rabbis realized that one shouldn't and couldn't wait for those rare moments of inspiration needed for prayers of self-expression.[160] So the Jewish prayer praxis was based on a set liturgy with short moments only for spontaneous, personal reflection. For example these moments have been inserted after one has finished the silently prayed Standing-prayer.[161]

Recording the prayers, however, was a process that took ages. It already began in the days after the Babylonian Exile (587-538 BCE). The tradition ascribes the first formulated prayers to the Men of the Great Assembly, a governing body of 120 persons, that functioned as such in Judea in a certain period during the Persian occupation (538-333 BCE). The phrasing of the blessing "Blessed are You, Lord, our God, Master of the Universe ..." is ascribed to them.[162] It is not certain, historically, whether such a body ever existed, but nevertheless this tradition shows that the set text of certain prayers is very old indeed.[163] The language of the prayers is, generally speaking, literary, not scientific. Resistance to writing down the prayers continued to exist, as a result of which the liturgy kept moving for almost a thousand years.[164] And still the Siddur, the Jewish Prayer Book, is open to change on the basis of new experiences.

Recording the prayers has yet another advantage: it may prevent some people from overdoing things during prayer. The rabbis warned against exaggerations in prayer:[165] "Someone who dwells excessively on praising the Lord, praised be He, is driven away from the earth, as is written (in the book of Job): "Shall it be told Him that I would speak? Or should a man wish that he were swallowed up?" (Job 37:20), and [as elsewhere is written in the Psalms]: "To You [Lord] belongs the silence" (Psalm 65:2). Those who wrote down the prayers were, when editing them, well aware of the dangers of exaggeration. They knew from the Scriptures that the dialogue between God and man should consist of "some words".[166]

In short, we can argue that there is not one objection to spontaneous prayers as they well up in our hearts, provided that the person who prays uses these impulses for him/herself only and doesn't press them on others. And there are also no objections at all against prayers in the mother tongue. But both forms of prayer can't replace the set prayers in Hebrew, because praying (*têfillah*) isn't asking, but listening, an exercise in the Torah way of life.[167]

Concentration and state of mind

A second aspect concerns the extent of concentration and submission one prays with. The one who prays doesn't say the prayers because of God but because of him/herself. It isn't about conciliating God. If one blesses God one does so to convince oneself of the fact that God is good, great, merciful and just.[168] That doesn't alter the fact that God appreciates our prayers.[169] The Talmud states that God even longs for our prayers. That is to say that the contact is mutual. God too, appreciates contact. But just because of the fact that the person who prays does so in the first place for him/herself, it is important to say these prayers with attention, concentration, intention, inner commitment, submission or orientation. And all this is covered by the Hebrew word *kawanah*.[170] The tradition supplies the text of the prayer, the one who prays supplies de *kawanah*. The texts are of all ages and of the people as a whole, but *kawanah* is a matter of the moment and of the individual. A prayer without inner commitment is a wrong prayer.[171] Therefore a suitable environment for prayer is advised, for instance a synagogue. The Jewish law disapproves strongly of all that distracts from concentration during prayer: joking, chattering, gossipping, quarrelling etc. In the service it's the cantor's task to be a driving force for the *kawanah*, the dedication of the congregation.[172]

The Jewish notion of prayer assumes certain ideas, not moods or needs. After all – even in other important fields of life – we won't be led by our mood when taking decisions and carrying them out. If one doesn't feel like praying, because one is occupied with other issues, one should liberate oneself of those issues. After all, prayer is for one's soul what food is for one's body.[173]

A prayer should come from one's heart, but it shouldn't depend on its mood. That's the reason why Judaism takes it for granted that the ability to pray should be trained.[174] Praying is regarded as an art form. A pianist must practice at set times, regardless whether he feels like it or not at that time.[175] Only by practising the piano he could reach such a high level that he could devote himself to it spontaneously. It's just the same with prayers: you should practice praying to be able to pray with *kawanah*.[176] So you should take your time for it. Pious Jews in ancient times rested an hour before saying their prayers in order to concentrate their thoughts on their Father in heaven. The Talmud states: "Whose spirit isn't quiet, should rather not pray".[177]

Individual and community

In Psalm 69:14/13[a] we read: 'But as for me, let my prayer be to Thee, O Lord, in an acceptable time'. In the Talmud 'an acceptable time' is explained as the time when the congregation is praying.[178] Though praying in the midst of the community regularly causes distraction, yet the rabbis prefer the community prayer to the individual prayer. That's the reason why they set a number of essential prayers which are only allowed to be said during a meeting of the congregation, that is to say, a company of ten or more adult Jewish men (*minyan*). The psychological factor is that sharing your experiences with a group emanates spiritual power. Also the tie with the people of Israel is strengthened as a whole. That is especially important as the Jewish people lives dis-

---

a   Dependent on the Bible translation which is used.

persed among the nations and is dominated by the non-Jewish culture.[179] The individual's welfare is, after all, very much interwoven with the well-being of the community, so that both are being experienced as identical. The Talmud reads:[180] 'A man should always link up with the community [even when he says a prayer all by himself during a journey]. How then should he say [his prayer]? May it be Your will, Lord our God, to lead us in peace'. Even someone who prays for his safety far away from his community, should not only pray for his own safety, but also for the safety of the group.

That's the reason why almost all prayers of the synagogue are in plural.[181] The communal prayer leads the one who prays to the needs and sorrows of his fellow man. For instance, the *Kaddish*-prayer, the prayer of those who are mourning, may only be prayed when there is a *minyan* (ten male adults). This prayer is a confirmation of lasting belief in the LORD even after the loss of a loved one. Not the contents – which have nothing to do with that loss –, but the reciting together comforts the mourners who may gather from it that others also mourn the loss of a loved one. In the eighth strophe of the Standing-prayer we read: 'Heal us, O Lord, then we will be healed'. So the prayer to be cured is also directed at the community. At the moment of prayer a link comes into being between the on who is praying an the other people who are ill.[182]

The idea of the *minyan*, the ten men needed to form a legal congregation, is rooted in the sense that people are social beings, and that through the presence of others the individual's consciousness is heightened.[a] Even he who prays alone knows that others are also praying at the same moment.[183] Man doesn't stand alone before God. He stands before Him as a member of the community. Our relation with Him isn't like the relation of one person, the I, to a You, but as a we to a You. In Judaism one never prays as an individual, detached from the rest of the world.[184]

---

a Think for example of the effect of joining in the laughter instead of laughing all alone, by oneself.

God, hearing our prayers

As we explained in the previous sections man should, ideally speaking, only be allowed to pray for God's help to reach noble ends. After all, not everyone is granted this high level of spiritual service. Far from it, ordinary people pray also for their daily needs and often make asking and pleading the heart of their prayer. This needn't be bad actually, because the really pious person addresses himself to God with all his worries, as do children that appeal to their parents. However, the petition- or question prayer can easily degenerate and even become vulgar. In such an empty prayer God is asked to hold up the natural way of things, the laws of nature, to comply with the wishes of the one who's praying. The Talmud gives some examples:[185] 'If the wife of a man is pregnant and he says: "Lord, grant my wife to bear a baby boy", that's an empty prayer'. The child's gender has already been determined and can only be altered by interfering in the natural course of events, and he shouldn't ask. The Talmud continues: 'If a man comes home after a journey and he hears cries of distress in the city and he says: "[God], please, let it not be my house", again, that's an empty prayer'. After all, if there is an emergency, it can only be taken away by running counter to nature and he shouldn't ask.

Some prayers are not only empty, but unworthy even and degrade praying to a demonstration of self-interest. That is the case with praying for victories at sports events or for having an easy exam. Most distressing however, are prayers that are nothing short of immoral. Prayers that attempt to stir up hatred between people and to encourage feelings of revenge.[186] In times of war people mustn't pray for victory but for peace, so that the Holy One, praised be He, will influence the hearts of both parties, so that they will make peace! Pious people will only pray to God for help to achieve the best in man.[187]

The above also leads to another view at the hearing of prayers. The sixteenth strophe of the Standing-prayer concludes with the words: 'Blessed are You, Lord, who hears our prayers'. It doesn't say: 'fulfils' or 'grants', but it says: 'hears'. The one who prays, can be certain of the fact that God is listening to his prayers, is concerned with it.[188] A prayer is heard when it gives us a feeling of God's presence, it's not heard when it has given us what we asked for. When God hears a prayer that does not mean that He'll make the world a fairer place by his intervention, but that He accompanies those who suffer. Who prays sincerely, doesn't ask God to change the world in order to make life easier. He only asks Him to be with him when he'll find himself in difficult situations.[189]

The Jewish answer to the question whether praying has any influence on what is prayed for, is not unambiguous. In the first place man should understand that he shall never be able to completely fathom God's creation: 'For My thoughts are not your thoughts, nor are your ways My ways' (Isaiah 55:8). Therefore man shouldn't play judge about God when matters are difficult to understand, e.g. in sickness and during persecution. In spite of that, man can be sure of God's all-seeing Eye and his strict justice (Psalm 94). You should assume that even in hopeless situations salvation could be near (2 Samuel 12:22). For instance when someone is mortally ill: perhaps a miracle will happen, perhaps the doctors have erred, perhaps a therapy or medicine will be invented. And when the patient's situation worsens, it's about realizing relief of the patient's suffering. As long as he's alive, pious people should invoke God's help.[190] But faith healing solely by the power of prayer isn't recognized in Judaism. They pray God whether He will make the doctors heal the patient, whether He will grant them the correct insight in time, so that they will be able to make a correct diagnosis and use the correct therapy.

And of course, God may be asked for health in a preventive sense, for His help when trying to lead a healthy life (Exodus 15:26). And for a certain income, God may be asked for as we read: 'Grant us an honourable way to earn our daily bread'. Food and means of sustaining life are asked 'from God's hand', so that we will be independent (1 Chronicles 29:12). Don't ask for wealth, and certainly not at the expense of other people, but only ask for your daily bread (Proverbs 30:8). Because the main issue here are sufficient means of sustenance, so that you'll be able to lead a dignified life, and it's not about being or becoming rich.[191] And again, such a prayer is an assignment to provide for yourself and to help other people who won't be able to do so.

Prayer and Sacrifice

Prayer is, in the Jewish tradition, the fulfilment of the task of serving God "with all your heart and with all your soul" (Deuteronomy 11:13). The Hebrew word for 'to serve' or 'service', *avodah*, was originally used for the temple-service. After the Babylonian exile it was used for the "service of the heart" (*avodah halev*), i.e. prayer.[192] In the Septuagint the word *avodah* was translated with the Greek word *leitourgia*, and from then on the term 'liturgy' denoted everything connected with religious practice and prayer.[193]

Already in Tanakh (the Hebrew Bible) the sacrificial service and prayers existed next to eachother. Abraham built altars, but also asked God for law and justice. Channah (Hannah) prayed to God in the tabernacle of Siloh, and what she said has been handed down in 1 Samuel 2:1-10. And of course the Psalms served in the Temple as set prayers and thanksgivings for joint and individual use. Not until the Babylonian exile (587-538 BCE), after the destruction of the Temple in Jerusalem, a situation arose in which prayers gradually began to come into the place of the sacrificial service.[194] After the destruction of the second Temple in 70 CE the same situation occurred again and the liturgy of the synagogue was extended with various reminders of the sacrificial service.

It's often said that the prayers in the services in the synagogue replaced only after 70 CE the then lost sacrificial services. But the experience that study and prayer could be an addition to or even an alternative for the sacrificial service, which tried to bring about the contact between God and man, must be much older. After 70 CE the rabbis should've never been able to bring the Standing-prayer and other liturgical elements in line with the sacrificial service, hadn't these matters already been considered forms of "sacrifice-less" religious service in the days of the Temple.[195] Prayer and sacrificial service have always been closely connected and this will always remain.[196]

The liturgy of the synagogue fits in directly with de liturgy of the second temple, which before 70 CE consisted of prescribed prayers and songs of praise for the priests, used to interrupt the cultic activities of the morning sacrifice. There was a similar liturgy for the "representatives of the people". Every week a delegation from the various districts went to the Temple to represent the people of Israel for a week at the sacrificial service. It was each district's turn twice a year. In the district towns meetings of those who'd stayed at home took place with a liturgy of its own, that linked up closely with the sacrificial service.[197] Two of the three daily prayer times coincided with the times of the daily sacrifice: the morning-prayer (shacharit) with the morning sacrifice, the afternoon-prayer (minchah) with the afternoon sacrifice.[a] Especially the Pharisees rendered the ritual symbolism of the sacrificial service into the liturgy of the synagogue.[198]

Other forms of worship

Other forms of worship (avodah) have been looked for as well, next to the sacrificial service and prayer. One of them is the study of the Torah. The Jewish worship embraces the study of the Torah. Many Jewish scholars study the Torah wearing their prayer shawls (tallit) and their phylacteries (têfillin). The study of the Torah is a central element in the synagogue service and the reading of the Torah was and is a set part of the service on sabbath, Monday and Tuesday. Exegesis too, is an ordinary part of the services, though not essential. Reciting the Hear-Israel-prayer in the morning and in the evening is put on a par by Rabbi Jeshu'a (1st century CE) with studying the Torah day and night.[199] This point of view could be understood if we realize that this prayer isn't a prayer, strictly speaking. As we already saw, it's not

---

a This sacrifice (Hebrew: minchah) even gave its name to the afternoon prayer.

addressed to God, but to Israel and contains important texts from the Torah.

There are two reasons why Torah-study is also seen as a form of worship. In the first place man returns to Sinai, by means of studying the Torah, to come into contact with God. A second reason coincides with man's spirit and conscience, two matters he has in common with God.[200] In Judaism there is no mediator but a learning process between God and man. Religion and religiosity are not the contents of that learning process, but they themselves are the learning process.[201]

A third form of worship, next to Torah-study and prayer, is performing acts of friendship (*gêmilut chassadim*).[202] The next chapter will be devoted to this.

Sanctifying God's Name

The highest aspiration in Judaism is sanctifying God's Name, the *qiddush hashem*, in word and action, in life and if the worst comes to the worst, in giving up life, amidst a world in which the expediency of nations and people almost always tip the balance. So that some time or other the entire world will come to realize that He is holy, and that the kingship of heaven (*malchut shamajim*) will soon become a reality.[203] The sanctification of the Name of God as meant here, does not only consist of glorifying Him with words, but especially with actions. Making something holy (*qiddush*) means in Hebrew literally "to set something apart". It's about how people are going about with eachother. Making yourself 'holy', doesn't mean secluding yourself from a wicked world in order to be able to live more piously. If you want to live according to the Torah you should behave in a way that differs from the accepted way of things. This won't make you popular: your behaviour causes your isolation, you'll be 'holy', by what you do.

A special form of the sanctification of the Name of God is reciting the *Kaddish*-prayer by those who mourn the loss of a relative. This act of sanctification shows that the faith in God will survive the loss of the deceased loved one.[204]

God's exaltedness and nearness

Two opposite feelings are very important for our relation with God: love (*ahavah*) and reverence or awe (*jirah*).[205] On the one hand we imagine God as great, exalted, terryfying and on the other as close, affectionate, and merciful. Both sides are linked inextricably. Loosen one of the other and it may lead to the wrong track.

Having an eye for His justice and greatness only, can lead to a paralysing fear of an offence, or to the understanding that He doesn't bother with the life of every day. The idea of His elevation can lead to feelings of littleness, insignificance, failure, desperation, despair. Too strong a feeling of guilt strikes one down, paralyses and kills. However, God doesn't long for the bad guy's death, but that he will return from his wicked path and stay alive. Prayer (*têfillah*) could be a support in the inner fight against negative feelings and thoughts. It can give the one who prays, the support of God's love and nearness in the fight against feelings of despair and the evil inclination (*yetzer hara*). God knows: "For [there is] not a just man on earth who does good and does not sin" (Ecclesiastes 7:20). He judges man according to his fight against the evil inclination.

On the other hand, only having an eye for the love of God and His mercy may lead to indifference towards sin and error: God will forgive, whatsoever, is the idea. To prevent exactly that, the combination of both aspects of God – exaltedness and nearness – and of both feelings of man – reverence and love – is essential for the Jewish idea of the relation between God and man.ª The rabbis think that man's posture during some prayers should reflect this idea. Reciting the blessings of the Standing-prayer one should bend one's knees when saying "Blessed" (*baruch*), one should bend forward when saying "are You" (*attah*), but one should straighten up before pronouncing the Name, "LORD" (*Adonaj*). During the Day of Atonement (*Yom Kippur*) one doesn't prostrate confessing one's guilt (*Widduj*), but only during the

---

a See e.g. Deuteronomy 10:17-18; Isaiah 17:15; Psalm 68:5-6.

prayers in which God's presence is experienced. At the Jewish New Year (*Rosh Hashanah*), when blowing the ram's horn (*shofar*), the broken tones (symbol of a broken heart) are followed by a long-stretched tone (symbol of completeness and cure).[206] Such polarities are characteristic for the Jewish attitude towards prayer and are also found elsewhere in Judaism, for instance at the polarity between rule and spontaneity, uniformity and individuality, law and freedom.[207]

Prayer and the image of man in Torah

At the end of this chapter some other observations regarding the relation of prayer with the image of man in the Torah. Prayer is the clearest expression of the dialogue relation between God and man, characteristic for the image of man in Torah. Without God's guidance man is 'a stranger in the earth' (Psalm 119:19). As a fellow worker of God in the creation man needs His help and may count on God's help, because God has willed man as a fellow worker. Therefore man's prayer is only directed to God, not to an angel, not to a saint, not to a mediator.[208] As we saw already the rabbis deduce the equality of all people from the story of the creation. That does not only imply that *everyone*

will be allowed and able to pray to God without a mediator, but it also means that *every man* is obliged to turn to God, because God asks him to do so.[209] Judaism has developed this obligation to a complex practice of prayer, which can easily be compared with art. To be able to feel the reality of prayer one should first develop the habit of saying prayers.

The pious man sees in the creation and in the mystery of life the hand of God. He discerns positive, moral powers at work in every field of human relations. He sees God's moral aims in the world of nature, in the history of nations and in the life of man. That's why he rejects every suggestion that the Creator shouldn't occupy Himself with His creation. The noble purpose of man's stay on earth is doing what God wants him tot do. The pious person is also a mystic at heart.

He doesn't expect the cosmic to be changed for his interest. Conducting a dialogue with God is to him or her a reward in itself.[210]

Prayer can make man's life more spiritual and may bring him to acts with a moral meaning. Prayers may help him to discover his orientation in life and can make him sensible for the ideals and aspirations of the faith. Prayers may bring man closer to God. An honest prayer may help to lighten fears and disclose new sources of power. A prayer (*têfillah*) helps man to be God's fellow worker in His creation.

4 Justice and Friendship

The Hebrew words I translated in the title of this chapter with 'justice' and 'friendship' are often rendered in bibletranslations with the English word 'mercy'. The English word 'mercy' is used in the verbal expression 'have mercy upon' and is synonym to 'take pity on'. These expressions convey the helpfulness from those who are doing well, towards those for whom things look bad. In Christianity 'mercy' is the translation of the Latin words *misericordia* (which can also be translated with 'pity') and *charitas* (which can also be translated with 'love'). Words like these play an important part in the orthodox-christian faith, especially in prayers. Afterall, the situation of man in relation to God is experienced as existential poverty, caused by the Fall, and this poverty towards God is experienced especially during prayer.[211,a] In the prayers God is implored repeatedly to have mercy upon man in his pitiful state. In answer to God's mercy the believer – in his turn – ought to love God, and this love should be made visible through love and charity for the fellow man. Reformational Christianity calls these acts of love 'the works of mercy'.

However, the foundation of human charity as "service in return" towards God's mercy resulted in the fact that the theological way of thinking about charity/mercy has always been very much concerned with the subject (the one who renders charity/mercy) and less with the object (the one who needs charity/mercy). Augustine (354-430 CE) and Thomas Aquinas (1224-1274) for instance describe charity in terms of virtues. Also within the Reformation this line of thought was followed and was God's charity for man taken as love not deserved. That's why the Reformers demanded not to base human charity on the needs of the destitute but on the change in inclination of those willing to help, a change by the power of the divine mercy

---

a   See also the discussion of the image of man in the orthodox Christianity in chapter 6.

This theology of charity and mercy in terms of virtues of the subject (the one willing to help) doesn't assume an equal relation between helpers and those being helped, and certainly not with regard to God's mercy towards man. Experiencing divine mercy is for man mercy not deserved, after all, he has no right to it, whatsoever. And because that model being the base of mercy and charity of men together, Christian theology traditionally was almost blind to the rights of those in need of help. It's true, mercy is seen as a duty of those better off to give, but not as a right of the destitute to receive. That's why for centuries the Christian poor relief had the character of patriarchal charity that conferred a favour of church or church associated bodies to the less well off.

Only in the second half of the 20th century the church and theology began – under the influence of social movements – to become more aware of what the less well off are entitled to.[212] But the theological basis of this right remains weak, as one sticks to the traditional ideas of the Christian faith about the relation between God and man in terms of existential opposites only to be bridged by God. In spite of the growing attention for the right of the destitute, unfortunately charity is still experienced very much by many Christians in terms of mercy, favour and virtue, more than in terms of right. This side of the idea of 'charity', coherent to the hierarchic character of Christianity, is – under the influence of the image of man in the Torah – not found in Judaism.

Right to social security

Judaism is egalitarian and democratic since the beginning of the Pharisean movement. It acknowledges mercy (charity) as a basic right of the needy, based on the Torah. The Hebrew words that best approached the meaning of "mercy", are *tsêdaqah* and *gêmilut chassadim*. The first can best be translated with "justice", the second with "acts of friendship". With it the support of the needy has been characterized, on the one hand as a right in the society, on the other as an event of reciprocity in personal relations. The duty to do mercy goes hand in hand with the right to receive mercy. Poverty, illness and death in general and in personal situations, have never been considered in Israel as fate, that should be suffered patiently.[213] They've always been seen as an assignment to act actively both for the person who's struck, as for his or hers neighbours. Experiencing this should lead to repentance or conversion. Confronted with this in a fellow man or woman, one's attitude should be one of benevolence and loving-kindness. And this not out of pity, but especially to fulfil a divine duty, not to receive some reward, but as an imitation of God (*imitatio Dei*), who – as we saw in the previous chapters – Himself supports those suffering and Who in the Torah granted the needy their right of social security.

Benevolence is not only an individual duty, but a matter of society as well, as the Torah is not only one person's textbook, but especially a textbook for the community. Within a Jewish community people found associations to relieve their mutual needs. They look after the poor, help bridal couples without means with the necessary means, enabling them to marry, provide orphans with food and clothes, ransom prisoners, visit the sick, bury the dead and comfort mourners, invite the pupils of scholars to their table and accommodate travellers. The homeless are cared for from "the petty cash", travellers from the "charger". Especially on shabbath the doors of Jewish houses are opened for those who won't be able to observe the shabbath themselves, and at a seder meal during Pesach guests are always welcome: "The hungry may come and eat; the needy may come and celebrate Pesach with us".

In this service to one's neighbour one realizes the service to God. Therefore one should render benevolence in silence preferably. And one shouldn't restrict oneself to one's own family or to one's own group. At Purim gifts are not only send to friends and acquaintances, but to the poor as well, even to the non-Jewish poor in the neighbourhood "for the sake of peace". Through the centuries Judaism has suffered enormous misfortunes such as crop failures, wars, economical crises. But those better off have always been more than willing to help the needy. They even had to be protected against giving too much, just to prevent themselves from impoverishment. And this benevolence is not just about the poor and the needy, but it's also about the sick, the dead and the mourners.

Acts of friendship

Some acts of mercy are called *gêmilut chassadim*, meaning 'acts of friendship'. The Talmud tractate *Pirkei Avot*, that summarizes Jewish ethics of the first century CE, reads in a statement I mentioned before:[214] "The world stands on three things – on [the study] of the Torah, on the service [of God], and upon acts of loving-kindness". All comments stress very much that this loving-kindness should be *done*. Put loving-kindness into practice, be benevolent![215] *Gêmilut chassadim* means: unselfish, practical acts of friendship[a] to boost the well-being of your fellow man.[216] Neither is it something that should only be done in deplorable situations. *Gêmilut chassadim* is about taking part in the joy and sorrow of your neighbour, rich or poor, healthy or sick. Characteristically social and age differences disappear. People will meet. Devote yourself to the other, consider other people's affairs more important than yours, that's what matters.

This personal form of solidarity has always been so important in Judaism, that it replaced the conciliatory effects of the sacrificial ervices after the destruction of the Temple. There is this well-known story about Rabbi Jochanan ben Zakkai (1st century CE) and his pupil Rabbi Joshu'a, who left Jerusalem after a visit to the devastated city.[217] Rabbi Joshu'a turned, saw the ruins of the Temple and exclaimed: "Woe is to us. This place where Israel's iniquities were atoned, has become useless!" But Rabbi Jochanan said to him: "My son, don't be sad. We now have another form of atonement just as effective as the former: acts of friendship, because it is said: "For I desire friendship (chèsèd), and not sacrifice; and the knowledge of God more than burnt offerings" (Hosea 6:6). A rabbinic exegesis of Micah 6:8 fits in with this story. The Micah text reads: "He has shewed you, O man, what is

---

a   Often translated in English with 'loving-kindness'.

good; and what does the Lord require of you, but to do justly, and to love friendship (chèsèd) and to walk humbly with your God?" On the basis of this text, in which three things are mentioned, which God asks man to do, it is said that mercy (acts of friendship) form a third part of the religion. The rabbi's maxim has always been that willingness to help those who need it is a sign of the true Israelite and of true humanity.[218]

Charity

The concept of "acts of friendship"(*gêmilut chassadim*) is very closely related to the notion of "charity", formulated as one of the most important assignments in the Torah: "But thou shalt love thy neighbour as thyself: I am the Lord" (Leviticus 19:18). This verse can also be translated with: "Love your neighbour, because he is like you".[219] This translation fits in with a passage in the rabbinical literature.[220] Here Rabbi Akivah, one of the greatest scholars in the first half of the 2nd century CE, observes about this text: "This is the basic principle in the Torah". The learned Ben Asai, however, responded with the words: "There is a more important principle, that is: 'This is the book of the generations of Adam. In the day that God created man, in the likeness of God made he him' (Genesis 5:1)". With this remark Ben Asai takes this notion of charity back to its basis: the fact that God created man in His likeness. From this idea stems the universality of the Jewish charity, which includes Jews and non-Jews, friend and foe.

The one God can't have created two kinds of humans. And so, in the Torah we read some verses after Leviticus 19:18 that charity is also for the stranger: "The stranger who dwells among you shall be to you as one born among you, *and you shall love him as yourself*" (Leviticus 19:34).[221] Almost all Jewish scholars from all generations agree, that Leviticus 19:18 is the basis of the entire Hebrew Bible.[222]

In Hebrew the verb *ahav* is used for "to love". Contrary to hate, love is an involvement that stems from positive feelings towards the ups and downs from the one you love. To love someone goes hand in hand with the pursuit to enhance the well-being of the "loved one".[223] So loving someone asks for acts of love, that is, both doing positive acts and refraining from negative acts. About loving your neighbour the Talmud says for example:[224] "In 36 places the Scripture forbids each and every humiliation of a stranger, if only with humiliating words." And elsewhere the Jewish scholar Reish Lakhish is quoted (3rd century CE):[225] "Bending the stranger's rights, means bending God's rights." This attitude does not only concern the stranger settled in Israel, "your stranger who is within your gates". The assignment "to love thy neighbour" also concerns the wandering stranger. This traveller is called "the stranger in the marketplace" in the rabbinic literature.[226] The scholarly Abbaye (ca. 300 CE) says about this:[227] "Man should always be full of fantasy in his reverence to God, meek, suppressing his wrath and stimulating peace towards his brothers, his friends and all people, even towards the *stranger in the marketplace*, so that he may be loved on high and here below."

The Hebrew word for "neighbour" (*re'a*), which also means "fellow man", is derived from a verbal stem with the original meaning "associating with someone".[228] So your neighbour is someone with whom you are rubbing shoulders: the man or woman you'll meet in daily life. The Bible doesn't acknowledge the "distant neighbour" in the sense of the anonymous other person elsewhere in the world. Loving your neighbour is something that should happen in direct contact with your fellow men, their relatives, and in their circumstances.

Nowhere in the Torah the verb "to love" refers to the enemy, but there are some clues, indirect ones, that indicate that even an enemy, in certain circumstances, should be treated with acts of love. We read: "If you encounter your enemy's ox or donkey wandering off, you must by all means return it to him. If you see the donkey of someone who hates you fallen under its load, you must not ignore him, but be sure to help him with it" (Exodus 23:4-5). Elsewhere we read: "Do not rejoice when your enemy falls, and when he stumbles do not let your heart rejoice" (Proverbs 24:17). And hereafter: "If your enemy is hungry, give him food to eat, and if he is thirsty, give him water to drink, for you will heap coals of fire on his head[a], and the Lord will reward you" (Proverbs 25:21-22).

Also in the Talmud you can come across texts which point to the same direction. There is this story[229] about Rabbi Meir (2nd century CE) and his learned wife Bêruriah once living next to some unsavoury people who constantly tormented Rabbi Meir, who prayed that they might die. When she heard this, his wife Bêruriah said: "How does this occur to you? Perhaps you find support in the psalm-verse: 'May *sinners* be consumed (from the earth)' (Psalm 104:35)? But it doesn't read *sinners* but *sins*![b] Besides, the end of that verse reads: 'And the wicked be no more'. As soon as *sins* have disappeared, there won't be any wicked people. So you'd better pray for them to repent and there won't be any wicked people left." Then Rabbi Meir prayed for them and they repented.

Charity nor love for one's enemy lead to the removal of a justified punishment for someone guilty. For society would deteriorate into anarchy. This appears from the connection of the word "neighbour" in Leviticus 19 with the verses 18 and 15. The 15th verse reads: "In righteousness you shall judge your neighbour". Real love for your neighbour is characterized in the administration of justice in a careful assessment of the question of guilt and punishment. Neither the assignment to love one's neighbour, nor the love for one's enemy are meant to deal rashly with injustice in the society. On the contrary, they're meant to protect the weak. This also goes for *gêmilut chassadim*, which may not lead to turning a blind eye to injustice and misconduct being forgiven without repentance.

---

a   The expression "heaping coals of fire on someone's head" means, that one tries to reform someone and make him repent. This expression has nothing to do with "shaming someone" or even "judging someone morally".

b   In the unvocalized Hebrew from Rabbi Meir's days, the word chatta'im (sinners), can also be read as chata'im (sins).

Justice

Next to "acts of friendship" and "charity", there is the idea of "justice", in Hebrew designated with the word *tsêdaqah*. In the Hebrew Bible this is the general term for justice. In the rabbinical literature it gradually gets the meaning of material help for the less fortunate in the society, poor relief. *Tsêdaqah* is more about anonymous and structural help, whereas *gêmilut chassadim* is more about personal help in individual needs. But a dividing line can't always be drawn. However, we can read in this literature that acts of friendship (gêmilut chassadim) are bigger than acts of justice (tsêdaqah),[230] because one does justice to the living only, acts of friendship to the living and the dead. One does justice to the poor only, acts of friendship to the poor and rich alike. One does justice with one's possessions, acts of friendship with one's possessions and with one's person. Acts of friendship spare the feelings of the poor (e.g. by lending them money in stead of giving), but in the case of justice the poor will feel ashamed to accept money.

Without any doubt its background is that in many cases acts of friendship are more difficult to perform because of their personal character than the more anonymous justice and poor relief. Acts of friendship are "held in higher regard" because they don't consist of material help only, but because one does so from one's heart: it's about sympathizing with one's fellow men.[231] *Tsêdaqah* can be done anonymously. Donating money to charities is – for instance – a form of justice that can easily be done in anonimity. *Gêmilut chassadim* on the other hand, is aimed directly at those people who need it: visiting the sick, attending funerals, celebrating weddings, acts that are always personal and that demand a bigger effort than the more anonymous *tsêdaqah*.

In the following paragraphes I'll briefly discuss a number of aspects of justice and acts of friendship and show how Judaism traditionally gave shape to them. First to come up are the attitude towards slavery, work ethic and supporting the poor as examples of justice (*tsêdaqah*). After that visiting the sick, supporting the dying, burying the dead and comforting the mourners pass in review as acts of friendship (*gêmilut chassadim*).

Protecting the slaves[232]

In the Graeco-Roman, the Celtic and the Germanic cultures the division of labour was part of a system of class distinction, discrimination and oppression of the social and economical weak. Freedom, equality and authority were reserved to the higher circles of the nobility, the clergy and the free citizens. For centuries the economic and social relations were defined by a feudal system that considered slave labour and serfdom were very usual things. Economically seen, sectional interests and enrichment at the expense of other people predominated everywhere. Starting from the rules of conduct of the Torah, the rabbis have always opposed this unbiblical society, often by means of their personal way of life.

Equality is not a matter of course. In ancient times slavery was so common, that Plato and Aristotle could equate slaves with animals. In a world of that kind there is no place for mutual responsibility, solidarity, pity and sympathy. The Torah's point of view couldn't be more different. The less rights a slave had in ancient times,[a] the more the Torah protects him. When a master knocked his slave but one tooth, he was free. Slaves should be treated with respect and dignity. According to the Jewish law a master didn't have the right to give his slave a humiliating task. He was not allowed to make him do tasks, he wouldn't do himself. He wasn't allowed to adopt the attitude of a superior.

He wasn't allowed to order him to tie his shoelaces or to carry his clothes to the bathhouse, because these servile jobs were not considered to be in accordance with the slave's personal dignity. A slave was not allowed to be sold at a slave market. A sale should be dealt

---

a   Slaves were at the mercy of their masters. However, some slaves were treated well. E.g. some were kept as teachers for the children of their master.

with in silence and dignity. The slave became part of his master's family and was entitled to the same food. During the time the slave served his master, the master was obliged to maintain the slave's family. The master was not entitled to take any advantage of the income of the slave's children or wife.

The medieval Jewish scholar Nachmanides (1194-1270) stresses the undesirability of any slavery in the light of the first of the Ten Commandments: "I am the Lord, your God, who brought you from the land of Egypt, from the house of slavery" (Exodus 20:2). To Nachmanides this means: "As I freed you from slavery, you don't have the right to enslave others". Slavery in general is – in Judaism – considered undesirable: "Because they are *My* servants" (Leviticus 25:42). Cruelty towards slaves is worse: "You must not rule over him harshly, but you must fear your God" (Leviticus25:43).

Entirely in agreement with the image of man in the Torah, the Torah prescribes that slaves should be set free after some time. The idea is that each member of the national community will be economiccally independent. This, however, has not always be possible. In biblical times, for instance, a thief could be sold into slavery by the court of justice, if he proved not to be able to return the stolen goods or its value. The retail price was payed to the person robbed. Also someone too poor to support himself and his family, could sell himself into slavery. To prevent relapse into poverty, the Torah demands that the slave at his release after the set time, had to be provided with a considerable amount of money by his former master: "If you set them free, you must not send them away empty-handed. Remember that you were a slave in the land of Egypt and the Lord your God redeemed you. Therefore, I am commanding you to do this thing today" (Deuteronomy 15:13-15). According to the Talmud the master had to provide the slave with things worth thirty *sela* at least as a "golden handshake", in those days a substantial sum. These 'things' should consist of seed or cattle, possessions that could yield profit. In that case the freed man should be able to build again an economically independent life.

According to Rabbi Moshe Alshich (16th century) the aim of slavery in the biblical sense is primarily positive: the master should help his servant to take his first steps on the path to a financial, economical, social and personal independence. After all, if he should send back his slave to the society in the same financial circumstances as those in the beginning of his servitude, in fact his master didn't contribute anything at all to his rehabilitation. Later we'll happen upon the same idea with regard to the poor.

The work ethics of the Torah[233]

Work is an important pillar in every society and so a necessary condition for bringing about a fair society. But work alone doesn't bring about this fair society automatically. Therefore it should be accompanied by – among other things – work ethics based on mutual trust and honesty. Honesty is an important aspect of the work ethics of the Torah and is emphasized in Judaism as a leading principle especially in the world of business. The Torah and the Talmud contain many provisions and stories to encourage honesty in employment and trade. One of those stories is about the charicmatic Abba Chilkiah (1st century), who was known for God hearing his prayers for rain. Once there was a great draught in the land and the Torah-scholars sent some envoys to Abba Chilkiah. When they arrived, he was just working as a day labourer in the fields, but he didn't even greet the envoys. In the evening they asked him why and he answered: "I was hired as a day labourer and didn't greet you, because I didn't want to interrupt my work and in doing so would steal from my employer."[234]

In the eyes of the rabbis work is in principle an honourable activity. Many great rabbis in the first centuries CE practised in a simple trade. For instance, Rabbi Jochanan (2nd century CE) was a cobbler and Rabbi Yitzchak (2nd century) was a smith. Work is also the basis of pursuing charity (tsêdaqah).

Then work becomes more than only supporting oneself or increasing one's wealth. By donating to charity, someone's business or employment is sanctified and all earthly things get a sacred character. Even though only a part of one's income is put into charity, yet one raises – by doing so – the rest of one's income and its sources above the ordinary. Man creates as it were an abode for the Most High in the everyday life.[235] In the Talmud charity is compared with all sacrifices.[236] Elsewhere in the old rabbinical writings we read that justice and acts of friendship equal all commandments of the Torah.[237] Donating money or goods to good causes puts human labour on a higher plane.

Charity and justice, however, may have their drawbacks, if one is blind to the question how the poor have become poor. In that case one runs the risk of creating a dependent group of the poor, that is going to live off (the) society. Poverty is no longer fought effectively, because citizens are no longer taught to stand on their own two feet. Subsequently more and more people withdraw from employment and start living on allowances and charity.[a] But the Talmud does speak about an imperative work ethic, in the sense that an attitude, in which dependency of the support of others is central, is rejected. Concerning this Rabbi Akiva says:[238] "You should rather celebrate shabbath as plainly as any other weekday, than becoming dependend on the charity of others". For the donor this means that in helping other people, he should try to make them self-reliant financially. Maimonides (1135-1204) takes the view that someone who runs the risk of becoming dependent financially, could/should best be helped by providing him with a partnership, a loan or a job so that he needn't lose his financial independence. In the Hebrew Bible the care for the financial and economical independence of those without property, is an integral part of the religion.

Supporting the poor[239]

The Bible regularly points out the obligation to support the poor: to help them with material support, to give them donations and loans in

---

a   A social danger if and when social benefits are too easily provided.

cash or in kind and all this generously.[a] After all, the care for the poor, the hungry, the widows, the orphans and the strangers is a quality of God Himself (Deuteronomy 10:17-18; Psalm 132:15; 146:7), and man is expected to imitate Him as he is God's partner in the creation. The care for the poor is not a matter of course as shown in the following story from the Talmd, which sets the image of man in the Torah against the fatalistic image of man a lot of rulers in Europe and the Middle East had for ages on end.

One day Rabbi Akiva discussed with Tinnius Rufus, the Roman governor of the province of Judea, at the outbreak of the Bar-Kochba revolt in 132 CE. Tinnius Rufus accused Rabbi Akiva: "If your God loves the poor, why doesn't He support them?" Rabbi Akiva answered: "He doesn't do so, so that we, by helping them, can be saved from punishment in Gêhinnom[b]". "On the contrary," Tinnius Rufus argued, "this sentences you to the punishment in Gêhinnom, because by helping the poor you interfere with God's rule of the world. I'll exemplify this by means of a parable. Suppose an earthly king is angry with his servant, throws him into jail and orders not to give him any food or water, and someone should go to the servant and give him food and water. When the king should hear this, wouldn't he be angry with this person? And you are called servants, as it is written: 'For the children of Israel are servants to me' (Leviticus 25:55)." But Rabbi Akiva countered and answered: "I'll show you your wrong by means of another parable. Suppose an earthly king should be angry with his son, throw him into jail and order not to give him any food or water, and someone should go to the son and give him food and water. Wouldn't the king, on hearing this, send him a gift? Besides, we're not only called 'servants' but also 'sons', as it is written: 'You are sons of the Lord, your God' (Deuteronomy 14:1)." Tinnius Rufus countered: "You are called sons as well as servants. You're only called sons when you obey the Almighty. At this moment you don't obey the

---

a   Isaiah 58:7, 10; Ezekiel 18:7, 16; Proverbs 14:21, 31; 19:17; 31:20; Job 22:5-9; 29:12-13; 31:16-20; Psalm 37:21, 26; 112:5, 9.

b   I.e. hell.

Almighty [because you support the poor!]" But Rabbi Akiva answered him: "Isaiah the prophet says: '*Is it* not to share your bread with the hungry, and that you bring to your house the poor who are cast out?' (Isaiah 58:7). When should one bring to one's house the poor who are cast out? Now, at this moment!".

In the Torah several rules are given how to support the poor. For instance, in Exodus 23:11 the sabbatical year is established, "that the poor of your people may eat". Every seventh year the fields must not be tilled and their natural produce was intended for the poor. Leviticus 25:6 broadens this to all those in need, and mentions again the poor in the person of the day labourer and the stranger. And Deuteronomy 15 renders this seventh year also into a year of remission of debts (verses 1 and 2), and warns against witholding loans to the poor because of the seventh year being near (verses 7-11). The Torah also requires that the poor should be enabled to participate in the pilgrim's festivals (Deuteronomy 16:11, 14), which means that they should be enabled to participate in the sacrificial meals.

In the tax system in ancient Israel also legal provisions were made to support the poor. In non-sabbatical years twice ten percent of the harvest (the first and the second tithe) was to be reserved for special ends. The second tithe in the third year of the seven-years' period was meant for the poor, the Levite, the stranger, the widow and the orphan (Deuteronomy 14:28-29; 26:12-15). They could eat this second tithe where they lived.[a] This third year even took its name from this second tithe for the poor and is simply called "the year of the tithe" (Deuteronomy 26:12).

And each year there was the ordinance of "the corner of the field". In Leviticus 19:9-10 and 23:22 we can read that when the harvest was being gathered in, the corners of the field shouldn't be touched. Even everything that during harvesting had fallen on the ground or in the

---

a   This contrary to the second tithe from the other years that should be eaten in Jerusalem.

vineyard had to remain there to be gleaned by the poor.[a] Moreover, Deuteronomy 24:19-22 adds the forgotten sheaves of the grain harvest, the olives that were left on the branches after they had been beaten for the harvest and the grapes that were left after the first picking. There is a whole tractates in the Talmud called after the "corner of the field": the tractate *Pe'ah*. In it the care for the poor is worked out in detail. From this text in the Torah the rabbis gather that there are four gifts from the vineyard: odd grapes fallen during the harvest, forgotten grapes or bunches of grapes; what isn't harvested because it's part of the "corner of the vineyard"; and odd bunches that were too small for the harvest. There are three gifts from the field of wheat: odd ears fallen during harvesting; the forgotten sheaves; and the "corner of the field". From orchard there are (only) two: what is forgotten and the "corner of the orchard".[240]

Although the idea that the poor should be helped is found in the whole Bible, the book has no specific name for it. In the rabbinical literature this care for the poor is indicated with the word *tsêdaqah* ("justice" or "benevolence"). And indeed, the measures described above are *tsêdaqah*: they can be realized anonimously and have a structural character. As mentioned before the word *tsêdaqah* didn't originally mean "care for the poor", but "justice". By the choice for the word *tsêdaqah* the rabbis showed how they looked at the care for the poor: receiving it is not a favour but a right, giving it is not a merit but a duty comparable with the modern obligation to pay taxes.

This view teaches us that "the poor do more for those well-to-do [by accepting the gifts], than the well-to-do do for the poor [by donating gifts]".[241] The underlying idea is that all our possessions belong to God and He has authority over poverty and wealth. This principle is illustrated concisely in a story about the learned Rava (4th century CE):[242] "A poor man came to Rava who asked him what he used to eat. The poor man answered: 'Fatted chicken and old wine.' 'But,' asked Rava, 'don't you feel any qualms that you are a burden to society?'

---

a   The poor were allowed to pick this up immediately after the harvest for their maintenance.

'Well,' the poor man said, 'do I eat anything that is theirs? After all, I'm having something that is God's?!' At that moment Rava's sister came and gave the poor man a fatted chicken and old wine. Rava accepted this as a sign and he apologized to the poor man."

In the Talmud the care for the poor has been developed in prescriptions to see to it that it should become a permanent part of society. Poor relief is such a universal duty that even those living of it are obliged to give those who are worse off.[243] To be able to decide in practice about those who were or were not entitled to poor relief, one drew a line somewhere with regard to the poor's property, considering whether this property was or wasn't used to acquire income. Poor relief should also be given to the non-Jewish poor to maintain good relations with the non-Jewish surroundings. Next one established the order of people entitled to poor relief. Women precede men and relatives precede strangers when gifts are handed out. The general rule is that the poor of the own city go before those of other places, but an exception is made for the poor from *Eretz Yisrael* (the land of Israel) who go before all other poor.[244]

Also travellers in a strange city are entitled to poor relief if they are no longer able to care for themselves, though they may have wealth at home. Once gone back home they won't be obliged to pay back the gifts.[245] Besides, no one needs to sell off his moveables before qualifying for poor relief.[246] One even needn't sell one's houses and other possessions if one should be the worse for it because of prices being lower than usual.[247]

Spending 10% of one's wealth is considered a reasonable virtue, 5% or less is considered too little. However, the 2nd century rabbis put an upper limit to someone's income of 20% to spend to poor relief, in order to prevent him from becoming poor and – in his turn – dependent on the community's poor relief.[248]

The Talmudic rabbis paid a lot of special attention to the psychology of poor relief. This should take into account, for example, the circumstances people were in prior to their poverty. Illustrative in this respect is the story about Hillel (end 1st century BCE) who put a horse and a messenger at the disposal of a poor man who had been wealthy before. Hillel even went so far that he acted as a messenger himself, when he couldn't pay the messenger's fee.[249]

The rabbis paid also attention to the way the gifts were presented to the poor. Their basic thought was that everything should be done to prevent the poor from being put to shame. One should refrain from giving something publicly, and thus putting the poor to shame.[250] Giver and receiver shouldn't know one another, this is the best approach.[251] To realize this several solutions were thought of. For instance, there was a room in the temple called "the room of the silent". In this room those better off could place their gifts secretly, so that the impoverished from well-to-do families could get their upkeep here without being ashamed.[252] The Jewish-Babylonian physician Abba Umana (early 4th century CE), known for his bloodletting, is said to be so pious that he had put outside his house, at a place not visible for the public, a chest in which his patients could put the money they had to pay for their treatment. Who was sufficiently well-off should pay the full price, the poor paid less or nothing at all. Nobody needed to feel ashamed towards Abba Umana.[253] Another approach is to lend the poor money but to consider it to be a gift later on. One is even allowed to fool someone who's too proud to accept poor relief, pretending to grant him a loan.[254] Then again the poor man needn't feel ashamed, after all.

The great medieval scholar Maimonides developed a system, starting from the above thoughts, existing of eight levels of poor relief with an increasing degree of merit for the donors.[255] One shouldn't understand a system like that as a means of conceit for the donors, but as steps to the best form of poor relief. The highest level doesn't consist of giving donations, but of helping the poor to provide again for himself. This can be done to lend him money for the necessary investment, to make him a partner in one's own business, to get him a job or to offer him paid work. So the end is reached in a fair way because the poor needn't lose his self-respect.

Maimonides also advises each Jewish community to appoint poor relief administrators (gabba'e tsêdaqah), honest people of good reputation. They should collect money on shabbath's eve and divide it amongst the poor.[256] Special measures were taken to see to it that the collection and the distribution took place in all fairness. Actually, these funds were also used for the upkeep of strangers without means, to ransom prisoners of war and to provide bridal couples with a dowry. Not everyone, however, considered collecting money to this end as an honourable job. Therefore the rabbis explained, on the basis of several texts from the Bible, that collecting means for poor relief was a greater merit than giving donations.[257] Its meaning is, to teach people to overcome their embarrassment.

In spite of the fact that poor relief, if one is entitled to it, is a right about which one needn't feel ashamed, the rabbis yet advised to do everything to avoid making use of it. The suggested preferences are not to eat special food on shabbath or te wear special shabbath clothes, if, in doing so, one can prevent making use of the poor relief system. It matters very much that man should keep his freedom and self-reliance. Moreover a wise and respected man should better keep himself in life by doing manual work – even butchering unclean animals is mentioned[258] – than being obliged to live at the expense of the community. The greatest rabbis did manual labour indeed to get an income to stay independent.

From the above it'll be clear that, already from Talmudic times, the Jewish approach of poor relief sooner starts from *tsêdaqah* (anonymous support) than from *gêmilut chassadim* (personal acts of friendship), although the boundary between personal and anonymous help cannot always be drawn clearly. In later centuries too, Jewish communities, subject to the society and the culture they lived in, have always given form and content to the central thought that solidarity with the less fortunate is of essential importance for the life of individuals and families, for the survival of the community and the people and finally, for the common good of all mankind.

Visiting the sick[259]

In this and next sections I'd like to discuss some other forms of charity which fall under the concept of *gêmilut chassadim* ("acts of friendship"). To begin with there is the task to visit the sick and to help to precipitate the recovery process. This task is closely connected with the Jewish vision of body and health. Indeed, the body is seen as the temporary form in which man lives in this world, but yet this form, after all the carrier of his life, has an unmeasureable value. One's body should be kept as whole and healthy as possible, because it's the tool man should use to carry out his divine task. That's why it is an unconditional duty to strive for health. And this duty does not only concern one's own health, but it's also one's duty to advance the health of all members of the community.

It's not surprising in this respect that visiting and supporting the sick is considered a *mitzwah,* a religious duty or divine assignment. And the more unselfish this duty is fulfilled, the more agreeable the act of the *mitzwah* is to God. As seen earlier in the Torah, for example in Genesis 18, the Lord Himself gives the good example by visiting Abraham who is recovering from de wound of the circumcision. In de Jewish tradition this duty or assignment is called in Hebrew *bikkur cholim* ("visiting the sick"). A number of regulations have been attached to the realization of this duty. One should bring the sick man or woman something: a good mood, comforting words, a friendly handshake, an encouraging look. One shouldn't hinder the sick in no way at all, for instance by "playing the physician". One should inquire cautiously after the patient's health and ask carefully whether something could be done to assist the sick and improve his/her situation. But one shouldn't intrude oneself upon the sick, let alone making the visit an ordeal. The visit should be a relief for the sick and should, if possible, work for the better. It is said that in that case each visitor takes away a sixtieth part of the patient's disease. One shouldn't take this number literally but as an aid to stimulate, by means of visiting him, the patient's recovery or to relieve the burden of the disease.

Illness and certainly severe illness changes someone's status for the Jewish law. A very ill patient is relieved from all religious rules.

In that case it's the surgeon who lays down what the patient is or isn't allowed to do with the religious rules. The Jewish-legal literature gives the physician absolute say over the Jewish-legal doings of the severely ill patient. In that case the shabbath rules are cancelled, not only with regard to the patient, but also for all those who are working hard to save his life. Of course, the treatment of a slight indisposition can wait till Sunday, but in the case of a severe illness the treatment of the patient comes first. It's the same with the food laws. If it is necessary for the patient's life to use non-kosher food, it's not only allowed, but even obligatory. Because for someone who's in danger of losing his life there is one *mitzwah* only: his life must be saved. In a Talmudic discussion several texts from the Torah are quoted from which the intention can be deduced that saving a life should come first before the observance of the shabbath, although those texts don't formulate this explicitly. In the end one puts forward the text from Leviticus 18:5: "So you must keep my statutes and my regulations; anyone who does so will live by keeping them". The rabbis accept this text as irrefutable proof.[260]

So human life is almost endlessly valuable and everything should be done to bring about recovery. However, in Judaism one is fully aware of the fact that not everything is in man's power, but that in the end life is in the hands of the Lord, blessed be He. Therefore medical science and medicines should go hand in hand with the call for help. As we already saw in chapter 3, in prayers for recovery God is not asked to interfere in the natural processes. Judaisme doesn't know recovery through the power of prayer only. In a prayer for recovery one only asks God whether He will make recovery possible, or whether He will grant the doctors a clear understanding so that they can make a correct diagnosis and choose the right treatment.[261] So it's all about prayers for help, strength, courage and wisdom, and about taking the right decision. Therefore, when visiting the sick a short prayer is sufficient, if only the word *shalom*.[262, a]

In this respect suggestion is seen as a good medicine. Even with a severely ill patient it's generally better to remain optimistic about the possibility of recovery or lengthening the patient's life. Besides, one should realize that it won't always be possible with every patient to discuss everything concerning his situation. Depending on someone's resilience, or on what he will indicate he can bear, one can tell the whole truth or not. Also the religious attempts one makes for someone's recovery, are not always discussed with the patient. A general rule can't be given here, prudence and empathy for the patient is called for.

When the illness grows more severe and the patient's life is in danger, friends and familie could come together to recite psalms or to learn ("lernen"). These meetings are ended with a prayer for recovery in the above mentioned sense. In the synagogue the father or the son or member of the family can be called up for the Torah-reading or to say a prayer for the sick near the Torah scroll. After that something is donated to benevolence (*tsêdaqah*). One shouldn't consider this an attempt to "buy" recovery, but as an expression of concern with the patient's fate. After all, this attention, albeit at a distance, can have a beneficial effect on both the patient and the closest relatives, if only because after the service it is communicated to them.

Because God is seen as the master of life and dead, the death of a human being is, in the Jewish tradition, ultimately brought back to a decision of the Almighty, and this decision is nothing but a "death sentence". The fight of a severely ill patient against death is represented as a fight with an angel of death sent by God. He is waiting for the soul at the bed's foot, which is busily trying to free itself from the body's embrace. Then he will take the soul before the throne of God. But even

---

a   Shalom is usually translated with 'peace', but better is 'welfare', or 'may you fare well!". The word is also used as 'good day!'. (See the next chapter as well).

when the sentence of death has already been pronounced, it can always be revoked or be torn up by the Heavenly Father. In this firm belief family and friends continue (with) their religious attempts to keep the patient alive. The Talmud mentions four acts that can be done in this phase of the course of the illness: benevolence, prayers, conversion and even changing someone's name. In this last case prayers for the dying person are said in the synagogue, but one changes his or her name into the name of a deserving figure from the Bible in the hope that God will be prepared to see the patient as another person who deserves to live on. The patient is said to be *gebenshed*, which is Yiddish for *blessed*, and one hopes that when someone whispers this in his or her ear it will be beneficial. The danger of this procedure is that it can be carried out from superstition or even from occultism. Originally, however, it's an expression of the belief that faith can work wonders even in the field of medical science.[263] Even when science and experience have given up someone, one should never stop caring, hoping and praying.[264]

When the severely ill pious Jew has made a complete recovery one of his first journeys should be to the synagogue. There he will be called up before the Torah and says a prayer of thanks to the Heavenly Father. If it's a woman or a girl who has recovered, the husband or the father will be called up before the Torah and his wife or daughter should say a prayer of thanks in the women's section of the synagogue after the reading of the Torah.[a] Thus one expresses that one accepts again the restored life as an assignment from the hand of God for which one is grateful to Him.

Supporting the dying[265]

In spite of all the attempts to keep the patient alive or to lengthen his life, one should be prepared for the approaching death. When it becomes clear that the sickbed has become the deathbed, one shouldn't

---

a   This at least is the practice in orthodox-Jewish communities, in which men and women attend the service seperately.

leave the family alone with the dying person and the care for the patient has become a a labour of love by the community. In each Jewish community this charity is organised by the *chevra qadisha*, also called "Holy Society". They occupy themselves with, *gêmilut chassadim,* acts of friendship. After all, the services rendered to the dying are acts for which one doesn't expect a reward. This is after the rabbinic maxim that the reward of a *mitzwah* (doing a devine task) is the *mitzwah* itself. Who does the *mitzwah* is rewarded by it. A holy society is not an "order", and doesn't maintain ties with sister organisations in other communities. It only exist in the own Jewish community. It's done voluntarily by members of each class, although in bigger communities some permanent employees have been appointed for some tasks. The holy society takes over from the relatives the care for everything concerning the deathbed and the funeral.

The deathbed itself should be surrounded with as much dignity as possible. Outburst of grief in the presence of the dying, must, if possible, be prevented. Very carefully one should try to prepare the dying person for the approaching death, if the circumstances make this possible. Judaism after all, doesn't to deny death in the end, but to face up to it. The ideal situation would be, if possible, that the dying person experiences the dying process consciously as a return if his/her life to his/her Creator. Perhaps the relatives will speak with the sick person about any disturbed relations in the hope to restore them. Because the idea is that one should try to become reconciled with one's fellow man before leaving life, as the dying day is seen as a *Yom Kippur*, a Day of Atonement.

The dying person should, if possible, recite the *Widdui*, a prayer of confession of sin towards God, that plays an important part during the Day of Atonement in the synagogue. After that prayer he or she blesses the children once more by laying on hands an saying: "God may make you like Efraim and Manasse" (for sons), or "God may make you like Sarah and Rebekkah, like Rachel and Lea" (for daughters). After that the process of dying follows during which those present may hum softly various melodies or say prayers. And again, the ideal situation will be that the dying one should breathe his last with the word *echad* ("één"), the last word of the *Shêmah-Yisrael* Prayer: "Hear, O Israel, the LORD your God, the LORD is one". As soon as death has occurred, the dead person's face should be covered and the relatives make a small tear at the top of their clothes. Then the care for the deceased will be left completely to the Holy Society, the *chevra qadisha*.

Burying the dead[266]

Once death had occured, the body should be handled with the utmost care and respect. After all, as the soul's abode it was a "dwelling of God". The members of the Holy Society lay out the body that lies under a white sheet, because it isn't considered respectful to behold the body of the deceased. Even during the washing the body remains hidden from view. The coffin of unplaned wood and the coarse linnen shroud should be as simple as possible because each human is equal in death. Before a male body will be laid in a coffin, it will be wrapped in a prayer shawl (*tallit*). Some soil from Israel will be scattered across the prayer shawl and the face of the body. Before the coffin will be closed permanently, one of the four tassels (*tzitzit*) will be untied to make the shawl ritually unsuitable. After all, the dead man is relieved of his obligation to pray. It is considered "defying a poor man", if one should give him a ritually suitable prayer shawl he no longer can use.

Until the funeral one keeps watch over the body. In this room psalms may be sung and prayers may be said but one could also study, i.e. *"lernen"*. A small light will be placed on the coffin, which has been lit immediately after death has occurred to keep the memory of the soul of the deceased alive. When the funeral begins, this small light for the dead man's soul will be kept in the home of the deceased. It is a *ner tamid*, a permanent light. It'll burn for twelve months for parents, thirty days for other relatives.

The funeral procession passes, if there is nothing against it, the synagoge. A Jewish funeral is not characterized by floats and many flowers, but indeed by a great mass of people that accompanies the deceased at the last journey. Helping to bury the dead, the *lêvayah* (literally 'escorting'), is an important duty one should always try to fulfill. Who couldn't take part in the whole journey is expected to take some steps at least with the cortege and to wish the deceased: "Go in peace!". Who lets the cortege pass by negligently, Proverbs 17:5 applies to him: "The one who mocks the poor insults his Creator".

Although nowhere in the Torah is found the explicit assignment to bury the dead, another form of disposal of the dead is inconceivable in Judaism.[267] Cremation is not in accordance with the spirit how Judaism treats its dead. After all, the respect and the care for the deceased also means that the dead body shouldn't be affected without urgent reasons. Only saving a human life that is in peril of death or solving urgent judicial questions are exceptions to this rule. This is also the reason why in principle corpses aren't exhumed and graves aren't dug up: the dead persons rest is considered eternal rest in principle. Only for a re-interment in the land of Israel these objections are dropped.

The grave is dug on the day of the funeral, because it is seen as a "freshly made bed for the deceased". A graveyard is not a gruesome place by Jewish standards. It's even called "House of the living" because here, at the grave the memory of the deceased is kept alive. At the cemetery the coffin (aron) is carried as the Holy Ark (aron hakodesh) had to be carried in the desert (Numbers 7:9). On the cemetery and at the grave prayers are said. The entire ceremony is in the sign of resignation. If a funeral oration is held, it should only bring back good memories, but one should take care not to exaggerate. Because all that could raise irritation and nasty remarks with regards to the deceased, should be avoided. At the end of the ceremony the relatives and friends of the deceased fill up the grave. This should happen slowly and after at least three shovels of earth the spade is quietly handed over to the next mourner, because the deceased "should not be buried hastily". Finally one of the closest male relatives recites the *Kaddish* prayer, a praise of God and a public confession that the tradition will continue: the next generation will take over the service to the living God from the deceased.

Comforting those who mourn

After the funeral the life of every day should be taken up again. The duty to comfort those who are mourning (*nichum aveilim*) should already start when people leave the cemetery. As long as the deceased has not yet been buried, this duty doesn't exist. "Don't try to comfort the one who mourns as long as the deceased is in front if him," the Talmud states. But on leaving the cemetery those present line up in two rows, between which the relatives will walk and those present will say: "May He who is omnipresent comfort you, comfort you in the midst of all those who mourn for Tzion and Jerusalem," these being the first words of comfort.

Leaving the cemetery one is expected to donate money as *tsêdaqah* (care for the poor), because this should remind those in mourning of their responsibility for the world. Doing *tsêdaqah* is experienced as a remedy against the bitter sides of life. There will be alms boxes and all those present should contribute to the good cause. Finally one washes one's hands to – symbolically – separate death from life: one enters again the realm of the living.

After the funeral there will be a simple "refreshing meal" for those in mourning, prepared and presented by the neighbours or by the Holy Society (*chevra qadisha*), consisting of bread and boiled eggs. The guests don't sit down to avoid the impression of being guests at a banquet, moreover they should have taken off their shoes. Thus begins the week of mourning, the *shiva*, lasting seven days and kept for the seven kinds of relatives: father, mother, husband or wife, son and daughter, brother and sister. This custom goes back to Joseph's week of mourning for the deceased Jacob (Genesis 50:10). The one in mourning, the *avel*, won't leave the house in that week, but members of the community should come to visit him or her, to "sit *shiva*". Simply being there is enough in the first place, many words are not expected nor needed. On the basis of Job 2:13 there is even a rule that those in mourning should speak the first word at the moment he or she will be able to do so. And once again there will be ample opportunity to donate money for the poor and the deprived. During the times of prayer the *chevra qadisha* could organise services at the house of those in mourning. The restrictions of the week of mourning are only lifted for the shabbath. After all, this day is the "day of the world to come". Then the one in mourning could or should leave his house to visit the synagogue. On the last day of the week of mourning, a member of the Holy Society comes to visit the one in mourning for the last time. He bids the one in mourning farewell with the words of Isaiah 60:20 "Your sun will no longer set; your moon will not disappear; the Lord will be your permanent source of light; your time of sorrow will be over". Then those in mourning should rise to their feet and enter normal life again.

After the week of mourning a time of mourning will follow, a Jewish year of twelve months for a father or a mother, from the day of death. Thirty days for other relatives. One refrains from showing joy, and keeps wearing the ritually torn clothes, but for the shabbath. Only the rent may be repaired partially or sometimes completely. Also the *ner tamid*, the light in memory of the soul of the deceased, should be kept burning during the time of mourning. And the children should burn the *ner tamid* on the anniversary of their mother's or father's death, for twenty-four hours, all their lives.

Charity and the image of man in the Torah

As appears from the above, is in the Jewish tradition the idea of "charity or mercy" with its two aspects of *tsêdaqah* (justice or benevolence) and *gêmilut chassadim* (acts of friendship) a fundamental idea connected with the image of man in the Torah. In the rabbinical literature it is reflected on and developed till the details of daily life. Contrary to Christianity, where charity lies in the atmosphere of favours and virtues, Judaism has always considered this a matter of obligations and rights, based on Torah. Perhaps this approach could help our Western culture to reach a fundamentally new idea of charity.

5 Shalom is more than Peace

In the preceding chapters we saw that an important aspect of the image of man in Torah is that man is God's partner in the perfecting of the creation. In this chapter I'll find out what the Torah and the rabbinical tradition mean with this perfecting. The word 'shalom' plays a key role here, as it appears to convey the essence of a completed creation.

The Hebrew word 'shalom' has such a complex meaning, that it is almost impossible to render it in another language. This was amply experienced by the translators of the Septuagint, the Greek translation of the Hebrew Bible from the 3rd and 2nd centuries BCE. In this imposing work more than 25 different Greek words can be found as renderings of the word 'shalom'. The Greek word *eirènè*, 'peace', became the dominant meaning and with it came all kinds of shades of meaning from Hebrew it didn't have in classical Greek. So *eirènè* has become a typical case of "bible-Greek", that is to say, a Greek word of which the meaning has changed under the influence of Hebrew. When, for instance, David inquires after 'the *eirènè* of the war', literally 'the peace of the war' (2 Samuel 11:7)[a], the expression used there is utter nonsense in classical Greek, but derives its meaning from a Hebrew expression.

It's true, 'peace' has become the dominant translation of the word 'shalom' in the European languages, but very often one has only chosen but one translation out of the many meanings of the word 'shalom'. The Dutch word for peace, 'vrede', is cognate to the Dutch word for freedom, 'vrijheid'. Peace and freedom are closely connected in the German languages. However, in the Roman languages the word for 'peace' is connected with the word for 'treaty' as in 'peace treaty'. The

---

a   A translation like "and how the war prospered" (NKJV) makes the word 'shalom' entirely invisible. Later on we'll see the meaning of this expression.

Latin word 'pax' (peace)[a] is cognate with the woord 'pact' (treaty). Here we come across the source of the most important association the word 'peace' evokes with many people today, that is the absence or the end of war. The Hebrew word 'shalom', however, means a lot more than 'peace' in this common sense of the word.

The meaning of the word 'shalom'

So the Hebrew word 'shalom' is usually translated with 'peace'. However, this is after all but one of the many meanings and shades of meaning the word can have. That 'shalom' has a much richer meaning, appears already from the Hebrew verb stem 'shalam', from which 'shalom' was derived. The manifold meanings of this verb are: to be complete, perfect, healthy, reliable, solid, sound and fair etc.[268] And these meanings shouldn't be regarded as representing static situations, but especially in a dynamic sense, as ways of functioning. Forms of the verb 'shalam' are used for: a perfect and just weight (Deuteronomy 25:15), a complete reward (Ruth 2:12), a job that was done (1 Kings 7:51), a finished wall (Nehemiah 6:15), a finished house (1 Kings 9:25), a confirmed an performed counsel (Isaiah 44:26).

In many cases the notion of 'being whole or complete' provides a better understanding of the text than the notion of 'peace'. That's the case with Abram's vision, where we read that 'the iniquity of the Amorites is not yet 'shaleem' (Genesis 15:16). The translation 'the iniquity is not yet peaceful' is of course absurd. The translation 'the iniquity is not yet complete' does, however, have a real meaning. It denotes that this iniquity will drag on for some time. In another story we read that Jacob arrives 'shaleem' in the city of Shechem (Genesis 33:18). This means that he came 'safely' to the city of Shechem. Yet another meaning of the word 'shaleem' is 'to be *shaleem* with someone', i.e. to be loyal to someone.

Against the above background it's clear that the word 'shalom' will always have the meaning 'being whole or complete'.[269] Therefore the

---

a   Cf. French: paix.

meaning of 'shalom' can refer to 'the fact of being whole or complete', or to 'him or her who are being whole or complete'.[270] From this start(ing point) of wholeness or completeness, the word 'shalom' has then got a wide range of meanings. And it can refer to an individual or to a community. In most cases 'shalom' is equivalent to 'all is well' with him or her. So it depends on the situation which aspect of 'being well' is meant. Sometimes it's rather about safety than about peace, as for instance in Leviticus 26:6-8, where the word 'shalom' is used in connection with successful warfare. The text reads: 'And I will give peace [shalom] in the land, and you shall lie down and none will make [you] afraid [....]. And you will chase your enemies, and they shall fall before you by the sword'. In this context 'shalom' doesn't mean 'peace' but 'security', a security that even must be conquered by force of arms.

In many texts the word 'shalom' simply means 'good/well' in a physical and/or ethical sense, as is the case in the verse: 'Turn away from evil and do what is right! Strive for peace ['shalom'] and promote it! (Psalm 34:15). In stead of with 'peace' the word 'shalom' can often and better be translated with terms like 'prosperity' (in a material sense) and 'well-being' (in a social and spiritual sense). Thus we should understand the priestly blessing in Numbers 6:24-26:[271] 'The Lord bless you and protect you; the Lord make his face to shine upon you, and be gracious to you; the Lord lift up his countenance upon you and give you *shalom* (well-being)'.

Some people distinguish seven shades of meaning in the word 'shalom': prosperity, wellfare, reconciliation, security, peace, friendship, completion.[272] These seven however, seem artificial and don't reflect the ample meaning of 'shalom' completely. It can easily be supplemented with meanings like: wholeness, perfection, health, safety, deliverance and repose.[273] Sometimes it can even be translated with 'fairness' or 'righteousness', as in Malachi 2:6 the theme of which is justice and injustice: 'The law [Torah] of truth was in his mouth, and <u>injustice</u> was not found on his lips. He walked with Me in *fairness* [*shalom*] and *equity*, and turned many away from *iniquity*'. In all cases the word 'shalom' concerns good relations in the broadest sense of the word between people, families and nations, in marriages, or between man and God.[a]

It's obvious from the above quotation (Leviticus 26:6-8) that 'shalom' and war (Hebrew 'milchamah') are not necessarily opposites.[274] A well-waged war can even be referred to as 'shalom' in the sense of a complete or successful war (2 Samuel 11:7). One has 'shalom' in a battle when the enemy is beaten. David returns in 'shalom' after his rebellious son Absalom has been killed (2 Samuel 19:25-31). The text shows an ironic pun. De name Absalom, in Hebrew 'av-shalom', means '[my] father is shalom'. When David is met by the first messenger, his first question is: 'Has the young man Absalom 'shalom'? (2 Samuel 18:29). And it was this very 'shalom' Absalom wished for himself, but not for his father David, in spite of the meaning of his name (2 Samuel 17:3).

Of course 'shalom' means in certain situations also 'peace' as well, in the sense of the end of a war or there is no war on. That is for instance the case in 1 Kings 4:24[b], where it is told that king Salomo 'had peace on every side all around him', so that Judah and Israel could dwell safely and securely, living on the fat of the land. But for the most part the translation with 'peace' does no justice to the meaning of 'shalom'. For instance, God enters into a treaty of 'shalom' with Pinchas (Numbers 25:12) and with Tsion (Isaiah 54:10). It's almost always translated with a 'treaty of peace', but in both cases there is no question of ending a war between two parties. The treaty with Pinchas and Tsion should better be described as a 'treaty of welfare', an enduring relation intending the well-being of both parties.

The meaning of 'shalom' in a text like 'there was *shalom* between Jabin and the house of Heber' comes closer to 'peace' in the sense of an end to a war (Judges 4:17), though the meanings 'friendship' and 'alliance' are also possible here. In some texts 'shalom' does mean 'peace' as opposed to 'war'. For instance in 1 Kings 2:5 the shedding of 'the blood of war in peacetime' comes up. Sometimes peace (*shalom*) is in direct contrast to war or battle, as in Psalm 120:7 and Ecclesiastes

---

a E.g. Joshua 9:15; Judges 4:17; 2 Samuel 3:21; Jesus Sirach 26:2.
b In the Hebrew Bible 1 Kings 5:4.

3:8.These texts however, only are a minority among the texts contai-ning the word 'shalom'. Even when it's a matter of war 'shalom' needn't necessarily be translated with 'peace'. In Deuteronomy 20:10 the rule is that when one is going to wage war against a city one should offer peace (*shalom*) first. From the context however, one could gather that it's not about making an equal peace, but about subjection to prevent a disastrous end. Here 'shalom' means 'subjection' rather than 'peace'.[a]

Isaiah's vision of an era when there will be no war (2:2-4) takes up a very special place in the world literature. From the fact that in this vision the word 'shalom' isn't used, could be gathered again that 'sha-lom' is not the direct opposite of war. Anyway, this vision shouldn't be seen as a sign of pacifism. After all, Isaiah is too much of a realistic thinker who had also known the necessity of war under certain cir-cumstances (see e.g. Isaiah 28:6).

So essentially the word 'shalom' has little to do with the negative meaning of the word 'peace' in the sense of 'the absence or ending of war'. In a world of friends and foes – and the world of ancient Israel was like that – 'shalom' meant the complete harmony with friends and victory in war over one's enemies. Someone has got 'shalom' when he is successful in his undertakings. So the meaning of 'shalom' is always a positive one. The word always expresses fellowship with other peo-ple and the foundation and victory of life. 'Shalom' always expresses what is good and when there is no 'shalom', there is no good (see e.g. Lamentations 3:17). We can also see the connection between 'shalom' and 'tovah' (the good) in Isaiah 52:7. It reads: "How delightful it is to see approaching over the mountains the feet of a messenger who announces shalom, a messenger who brings good ('tov') news, who announces deliverance." When Jacob asks the shepherds in Mesopo-tamia whether Laban has 'shalom', he asks them whether Laban lives in harmony with his family, whether he has a friendly relationship with the people around him, whether he is healthy and prosperous,

a   This is also the case in Joshua 10:1, 4; 11:19; 2 Samuel 10:19; 1 Chronicles 19:19.

whether he is successful in what he undertakes, whether his cattle prospers, etc. Having 'shalom' means that one is safe and sound. So the opposite of 'shalom' is not so much 'war', but everything that can disturb the wealth and well-being of man and the good relations within his community.[275]

These positive associations of the word 'shalom' are also connected with the peace offering (Hebrew 'shêlamim') that could be made in the temple in Jerusalem till 70 CE. Elsewhere I argued that the sacrificial service shouldn't be seen as a collection of ancient, traditional, obscure rites, but as a "theology of action".[276] One of the points of doctrine one expressed in the sacrificial acts, was the belief that man could reach 'shalom' by means of his cooperation with God. The sacrifice symbolizing this point of doctrine is called the 'peace offering'.[a, 277]

Leviticus 3 describes the rules for the peace offering. The peace offering is the basis of all community offerings, made by or for the benefit of a group of people. The peace offering was, in terms of holiness[b], less holy than for instance the burnt offering, the sin offering and the guilt offering. Every animal of the cattle and the live stock, both male and female, was admissible and suitable for the peace offering. But it should be a sound animal, i.e. without a physical defect. The blood of the animal was poured out against the altar as the expression of the belief that life is God's and doesn't belong to man. The best parts of the entrails were burnt on the altar as an 'agreeable odour' for the Lord, i.e. God's part in the meal. The priest that butchered the sacrificial animal, was rewarded with the brisket and the right thigh of the sacrificial animal. What was left after the dues to the altar and the priests, was returned to the sacrificer, to prepare a meal for the company of his relatives and friends with him and for the Levites present who belonged to his community. The meal should be prepared and eaten according to certain rules. Each peace offering should culminate

---

a   The word shêlamim is plural. The singular shelem only occurs in Amos 5:22.
b   That is to say, the special position of the offering in question in terms of specific rules in order to distinguish it from other offerings.

in a communal meal and during this meal the 'shalom' of God and man should be experienced.

The peace offering was a voluntary sacrifice, that was made at a special occasion, usually when a wished for situation had been reached after a problematic period. Here lies the link with the name of this sacrifice: 'shêlamim' can also be translated with 'a sacrifice that makes matters complete' or 'a welfare offering'. A similar situation occurred for instance at the reunion with family and friends after a long period of absence (1 Samuel 20:6). In some cases the peace offering was more or less self-evident, as for instance at the end of a military campaign (1 Samuel 11:15), or when a famine or the plague had come to an end (2 Samuel 24:25). Sometimes the peace offering is called a 'thanks-offering'.[a] In that case it also expresses the joy for something that was longed for and was reached.

To sum up, the word 'shalom' in the Bible means all kinds of prosperity and well-being, good health, security, contentment for an individual man. In mutual relations it means harmony. After all, the well-being of the individual or the community depends on it. Agression, enmity and strife are damning for this well-being. Outer and inner peace are here the essential conditions.[278] 'Shalom' is therefore one of the key words and notions of the Hebrew Bible and it plays an important part in the postbiblical Jewish way of thought accordingly.

'Shalom' in the rabbinical tradition

With the exception of 'justice' (tsêdaqah) 'peace' or 'well-being' is the most praised notion among the Talmudic rabbis.[b] No words of praise are too lofty to stress the importance of peace as an ideal.[279] According to Rabban Shime'on ben Gamliel (beginning of the 2nd century CE) peace is next to the truth and the administration of justice one of the three things on which the survival of the world depends.[280] It's the

---

a   Leviticus 7:12-13, 15; 22:29; Psalm 56:13-14; 107:22; 116:17; Jeremiah 33:11.
b   From now on I'll use the word "peace" more often, but always in its wider meaning, of which peace in the sense of "no war" is a part.

scholars' and scientists' task to increase peace in the world.[281] All important prayers in the liturgy of the synagogue end with blessing peace.[282] 'Shalom' is the usual greeting among Jews in all circumstances. It's even one of the names of God.[283] Rabbi Shime'on ben Chalaphtah (end of the 2nd century CE) once said:[284] "The Holy One, blessed be He, didn't find a vessel more suitable to contain Israel's blessing than [the vessel of] peace." For it is said: "The Lord will give strength to His people; the Lord will bless His people with peace." Peace is so important to people that even the dead need peace:[285] "Great is the peace, for even the dead need peace, for it is said: And you shall go to your fathers in peace (Genesis 15:15), and elsewhere: You shall die in peace (Jeremiah 34:5)."

But without a specific meaning 'shalom' is yet a rather vague term. That's the reason why, in the rabbinical tradition, it is closely connected with the Torah, the doctrine of God about how man should live best:[286] "Great is the peace for she is given to those who love the Torah, as it is said: Those who love your Torah have great shalom (Psalm 119:165)." But just like peace depends on the Torah, so is the Torah, for her part, also depending on peace. Rabbi Chizkiah (early 3rd century CE) puts it like this:[287] "Great is the peace, for it is written about all Israel's wanderings in the desert: 'And they travelled and camped' (e.g. Numbers 33:6). That means [the plural used in these texts suggests so]: They travelled in discord and they camped in discord. But when they arrived at the mountain of Sinai, they all became one camp, because it is *not* written: 'And there the children of Israel camped' [plural], but: 'And there Israel camped' [singular] (Exodus 19:2). The Lord, blessed be He, said: 'This is the hour when I will give the Torah to my children.' " The singular shows, according to this midrash, that there was peace among the Israelites at that very moment. Elsewhere in the Midrash can be read that God said at that moment:[288] "The Torah is peace entirely. To whom shall I give her? To the people that clings to peace."

So there is a dialectic relation between Torah and 'shalom'. 'Shalom' and the study of Torah are closely connected in rabbinical thought. After all, if you want to know how to establish 'shalom', you'd best turn to the Torah. But even the study of Torah can only flourish when peace rules. The close tie between the Torah and 'shalom' is so strong in the eyes of some rabbis that the sincere, unselfish study of the Torah produces, as it were, 'shalom' spontaneously. Rabbi Alexandri (3rd century CE) said: "Who busies himself with the study of Torah for the sake of itself, does not only make peace in the heavenly court, but also in the earthly court. After all, it is said: "Or let him take hold of My strength" [i.e My judgement on the basis of Torah], that he may make peace with Me [in heaven]; and he shall make peace with Me [on earth] (Isaiah 27:5)." The verse quoted from Isaiah is in context with God's judgement of the earth (see Isaiah 27:1), a judgement for which He, according to the idea of the rabbis, consults the heavenly court. That heavenly court administers justice on the basis of the Torah – just like the earthly courts. The two-fold mentioning of 'making peace' (in Isaiah 27:5) refers, according to Rabbi Alexandri, to two different situations: the first mention refers to "peace in heaven", the second to "peace on earth".[289, a]

According to the rabbis' idea, peace or 'shalom' was already inherent in the creation from the beginning. The way in which man was created – as one single individual (Genesis 1:27) – is based on this concept. This emphazises the unity of all people as well as the value of each and every individual human life. The Talmud expresses this fact as follows:[290] "Man was created as one single individual for the sake of peace among people, lest one could say to his fellow man: 'My father was greater than yours.' " Here we're able to see the close connection between the image of man in the Torah and 'shalom'. So pursuing peace is one of the most important commissions in Judaism, so important that it isn't tied to place, time and circumstances. Other commandments in Torah are only executed if and when the situation gives cause to it, but the peace commandment must always be pursued. Rabbi Chizkiah observed:[291] "Great is the peace, for it is said of

---

a   When a certain expression is mentioned twice it's always explained by the rabbis as referring to two different matters. They often refer the one to this world, the other to the world to come.

all commandments: "If you (will) see…" (Exodus 23:5), "If you happen upon…" (Exodus 23:4), and "If you come across…" (Exodus 22:6)]. That is to say: when a commandment comes into your hands [i.e. when the situations occurs], you are obliged to obey, but when it doesn't come into your hands, you needn't carry it out. But here [in the case of the commandment of peace] it's quite different: 'Seek peace and pursue it' (Psalm 34:15). *Look for it in your own place and pursue it in another place."*

Peace asks for an active attitude and should be pursued always and everywhere, even in times of enmity and war. In an elaborate story about Rabbi Jannai (ca. 225 CE) is told that making peace even balances a poor knowledge of Torah and the Jewish tradition:[292] "Once Rabbi Jannai was travelling and met a man in distinguished clothes. Rabbi Jannai [thought he was a scholar and] spoke to him: 'Would my lord grant to my request and be our guest? The man said: 'Yes!, I would'. Rabbi Jannai took him home and presented him with food and drink. After that he tried to get to know about the other's knowledge of the Scriptures, but he didn't find any. He also tried to get to know something with regard to his knowledge of the oral Torah, but again, he didn't find any. He then asked him [to give him the honour he was entitled to as a stranger]: 'Please, take the cup and say grace!' However, the other said: 'May Jannai say grace in his own home!' Than Rabbi Jannai asked him: 'Will you be able to repeat after me what I will say to you?' He answered: 'Yes, I will!' 'Well, please say: A dog has eaten its bread!' Then the other man jumped to his feet, grasped Rabbi Jannai and said: 'How's that? You want to withhold my inheritance?' Rabbi Jannai demurred: 'Well then, is your inheritance with me?' The other said: 'Once I passed a school and heard children's voices say: The Torah was given to us by Moses as an inheritance for the congregation of Jacob (Deuteronomy 33:4). It doesn't say: 'as an inheritance to Jacob, but as an inheritance for the congregation of Jacob [that is to say all descendants of Jacob. How dare you withhold the Torah from me by calling me a dog?]'. Rabbi Jannai said: 'What gives you the right and dignity to eat at my table?' He answered: 'All my life I didn't hear an angry word that needed be refuted, and never I saw two people fighting without making peace between them'. Rabbi Jannai spoke to him [with regret]: 'So many good deeds are found with you, and I have called you a dog!'. He then declared the following word applicable upon his guest: 'And to him who orders his conduct aright I will show the salvation of God' (Psalm 50:23)."

Shalom and truth

'Shalom' is so important even, that – in certain circumstances – it is allowed to bend the truth in order to keep the peace or to bring it about.[293] This principle does not only apply to the relation between husband and wife (or more general: man and woman), but to the entire spectrum of human relations: between man and his fellow man, among nations and for the entire universe. The rabbinical literature gives several examples in which this principle is used to explain bible pericopes, which – at first sight – contain a contradiction. When, for example, after the death of the patriarch Jacob Joseph's brothers fear that he will take revenge for their earlier crime against him, when they had sold him into slavery to Egypt. Therefore they send Joseph the message: "Your father gave these instructions before he died: 'Tell Joseph this: Please, forgive the sin of your brothers and the wrong they did'" (Genesis 50:16-17). But nowhere in the Torah such a message of Jacob's can be found. So it's 'a white lie' for the sake of peace in the family.[294]

The subordination of truth to peace is so important that even God acts accordingly. At least, that is the obvious intent of the explanation of Genesis 18:13, after the birth of a son was announced to Abraham and Sarah, in spite of their ripe old age:[295] "Great is the peace, because the Lord, blessed be He, changed the words [of Sarah] because of the peace [between Abraham and Sarah]. For it is said: 'And the Lord said to Abraham: Why did Sara laugh, saying, Shall I surely bear a child, *since I am old*?' (Genesis 18:13). Great is the peace, because the Lord, blessed be He, changed the truth for it. Because first there was [what Sarah said] 'My lord is old' (Genesis 18:12), and then [when God conveyed Sarah's words to Abraham, it reads]: 'since I [Sarah] am old' (Genesis 18:13)." Sarah doubts the prediction and ascribes it to Abraham's old age, but God makes it appear to Abraham as if she ascribes it to her being old. And so the Lord, blessed be He, prevents dissension to arise between both spouses.

Also in the third example it is God who thinks up 'a white lie'. When God orders the prophet Samuel to go and anoint David as king of Israel, he protests: "How can I go? If Saul hears it, he will kill me" (1 Samuel 16:2). Then the Lord whispers a little lie in his ear: "Take a heifer with you and say, 'I have come to sacrifice to the Lord'." In the later Jewish tradition a discussion arose about this text. Shouldn't Samuel have trusted God's care? Shouldn't God have said to him: "Be not afraid, I am with you"? But others take the view that Samuel and God have acted sensibly, because one shouldn't endanger life and peace needlessly.[296]

In the attempts to make peace one may deal 'creatively' with the truth, too. We could gather that from a story about the first high priest Aharon who – in the rabbincal tradition – is the pre-eminent peacemaker:[297] "When two men were quarrelling, Aharon went up to the one, sat down in front of him and said: 'My son, see what your neighbour [the one you are quarrelling with] says. He torments himself, rends his clothes and says: 'Woe is me, how can I lift up my eyes and look my neighbour [whom I am quarrelling with] in the eye? I feel ashamed, because I behaved badly towards him'.' And Aharon stayed with the first until this one had removed the enmity from his heart. Then Aharon left and went to sit in front of the other one and did the same thing. And when they met later on, they embraced and kissed."

However, all this doesn't mean that one's free to tell easy lies appealing to peace. Also speaking the truth, voicing critcism, is – in many cases – an assignment of the Torah. Withholding the truth can easily lead to gossip and resentment. "Do not hate your brother in your heart, but you should reprove him", says Leviticus 19:17. Speaking the truth can also have a wholesome influence and withholding it can obstruct the true 'shalom'. A good example is for instance Abraham's attitude towards Avimelech, who wants to enter into a treaty of friendship with him (Genesis 21:22-27). To test his true intentions, Abraham chides him because of his servants' wrong conduct. Avimelech's reaction is positive and so the treaty can be made (verse 27). "Peace that isn't attended by criticism, is no peace", is also a legitimate point of view in the rabbinical literature.[298]

What is wise in what situation can not be said beforehand with certainty. The assessment of truth and peace should be made again and again. But who's conscious of the problem and has practised the examples that come up from the Bible and the rabbinical tradition, will perhaps be able to reach a good decision more easily.

Shalom and justice

In the mean time there are also in this world, in which 'shalom' is often a long way off, a number of problems to solve. The question presents itself which approach is best, generally. Rabbi Shime'on bar Jochai (halfway through the 2nd century CE) wondered why in the Torah the regulations for the civil society preceded all other ones. His answer was, that if there was a lawsuit between two people, there is a conflict between them, but once the court has decided, there will be peace between them. And peace is seen as a condition to be able to fulfil all other rules of the Torah. So in this view justice and jurisdiction are a necessary condition for peace. However, many Jewish scholars realized that even a judicial decision do not always restore peace. Yet, in theory, they supported Rabban Shime'on ben Gamliel (early 2nd century CE), that the world exists thanks to truth, jurisdiction and peace.

Not all rabbis however, trusted the administration of justice to reach peace. Rabbi Joshu'a ben Korcha (halfway through the 2nd century CE) came to the conclusion: "Where is justice, is no peace, and where is peace, no justice [is needed]". Mediation is better than the administration of justice, in his eyes that is. This point of view evoked in its turn fierce opposition of Rabbi Eliezer, son of Rabbi Jose the Galilean, who said: "Mediation is forbidden, and he who mediates commits a crime. Let the Torah drill through the mountain!" In other words: administer justice at daggers drawn.[299]

It is remarkable that the tension between making peace (to mediate) and the administration of justice has its origins in the opposite characters of Moses and Aharon. As I showed above, especially Aharon, the first high priest and brother of Moses, was considered the prototype of the peacemaker.[300] In that respect he is his brother Moses' antagonist, a Moses who personifies the ideal of justice especially. Another example of how Aharon operated in his attempts to make peace can be found in a saying of Rabbi Meir (halfway through the 2nd century CE):[301] "When Aharon met a bad person or an evildoer on the way, he greeted him in peace. When that man wanted to commit an offence the next day, he said [to himself]: 'Woe is me, how could I lift up my eyes and look Aharon in the face? I would be ashamed for him, for he greeted me.' And so that man decided not to commit an offence." Moses would probably have tackled the incident in another way, because just a bit later we read: "Why did *all Israel* weep for Aharon [after he had died], whereas *only the men* wept for [the death of] Moses? Because Moses judged strictly on the basis of the truth. Aharon on the contrary would never say to a man or a woman: 'You behaved outrageously'. Therefore it is said: 'And they lamented for Aharon, the entire house of Israel [men and women]' (Numbers 20:29). But about Mozes, who'd admonished them in harsh words, is said: 'And the sons of Israel [not the daughters] mourned for Moses' (Deuteronomy 34:8)." The discussion about what is better, the administration of justice or mediation is, just like the assessment between truth and peace, a discussion that among the rabbis had never been settled, but – depending on time and place – it was turned into practice.[302]

War and the making of peace

The biblical and rabbinical concern with the ideal of peace has always gone hand in hand with a greater measure of scepsis with regard to war. How unavoidable sometimes, war never embodies an ideal.[303] Yet

Judaism is not pacifistic in its approach of the conflicts in the world. It considers universal peace as an ideal that should be pursued but will only be achieved in messianic times. In certain circumstances beginning a war could be justified ethically or even be necessary. All ethics of the rabbis stay far away from glamorizing war. From this attitude stems the idea that a man is not allowed to leave his home on sabbath carrying arms. Yet if he had done so accidentally he is obliged to make a guilt offering in the temple.[304] The opposite idea that arms should only be considered as ornaments attached to clothes, was sharply critisized by the rabbis with the words: "Weapons are nothing but a shame. After all, it has been written: 'They will beat their swords into ploughshares, and their spears into pruning hooks. Nations will not take up the sword against other nations, and they will no longer train for war' (Isaiah 2:4)." One should imagine that the sabbath is seen as the "day of the world-to-come", the symbol of the messianic time, the completion of the creation. Carrying arms without absolute necessity is completely contrary to the character of the sabbath.

The attitude of Judaism towards war and peace is worded shortly but perfectly in the following remark:[305] "Great is the peace, for even in the hour of war we are reminded of peace."[a] Though sometimes unavoidable, in Judaism war is always seen as a breakdown of the attempt to solve a problem without violence. Therefore making peace is held in high regard.

A couple of times already I mentioned Aharon as the prototype of a peace maker. This image of Aharon also belonged to the motto of the great scholar and Pharisee Hillel. He was an early contemporary of Jesus and could be regarded as one of the founders of the present Judaism. In the important Mishnah-tract Pirkei Avoth ("Sayings of the Fathers"), a summary of the ethics of the early rabbis, the first saying of this good-natured, tolerant scholar that is handed down goes:[306] "Be among the disciples of Aharon, loving peace and pursuing peace, loving people and bringing them closer to the Torah." Humility, patience, love for one's fellow man and the pursuit of peace are important parts

---

a   Here the mention of 'shalom' refers to the war laws in Deuteronomy 20:10.

of Hillel's range of ideas. This however, was not at the cost of the strictness of the moral and religious demands he made on himself and others. This also didn't stop him to impose on man the full responsibility to work on his own perfection and on the welfare ('shalom') of the community. Man is obliged to make efforts for himself and for others here and now, without delay. That is the gist of one of his sayings that goes:[307] "If I am not for myself, who will be for me? And if I am only for myself, what am I? And if not now, when?"

Hillel was the founder of the later School of Hillel, a school of rabbis that was to become the mainstream in Judaism after the destruction of the Temple in 70 CE. The majority of the rabbis from the School of Hillel belonged to the peace party in Jerusalem before and during the Jewish War against the Romans (66-70 CE). Rabban Jochanan ben Zakkai was the leader of this School during that war. During the Roman siege he left Jerusalem because he didn't agree with the fanatic battle of the Zealots against the Romans. With consent of the Roman general Vespasian, he established a school in Javne. There the School of Hillel was to develop into a centre of spiritual guidance for the entire Judaism in the later centuries. In addition to Hillel and Rabban Jochanan ben Zakkai the rabbinical tradition knows yet another long row of peace makers to this very day, like the great scholar Leo Baeck, who, immediately after his liberation from the concentration camp Theresienstadt in 1945, exerted himself to protect his former camp guards against acts of revenge.[308]

In the rabbinical tradition one frequently reflects on the relation between 'shalom' on the one hand and contrasts, quarrels and discord on the other: "Great is the peace, because it is given to the righteous. Great is the peace, because the ungodly won't have a share in it."[309] Discord, so the rabbis teach, will end in disaster. The country will be devastated, the town divided in itself, will perish, and the house of study will become a house of idolatry, witness the following story.[310] "Rabbi Ammi and Rabbi Assi said: Didn't it happen in the synagogue of Tiberias that Rabbi Eleazar and Rabbi Jose were so divided among themselves, that they tore up a Torah-scroll in their fury? Is it imaginable that they tore up a Torah-scroll literally? Let us say, that because of their fury a Torah-scroll tore up itself. Rabbi Jose ben Kisma was with them and said: "I would be surprised if this synagogue shouldn't become a place of idolatry". And so it happened, later.

Yet associating with each other and living in 'shalom' does not mean, that one is not allowed to have differing opinions or discuss them fiercely. In a saying on the fervour of the discussion in the house of study I already quoted earlier[a], we read:[311] "Even a father and his son, a teacher and his student become enemies when they dispute the explanation of the Torah; but if they don't leave until they are friends again, then [Numbers 21:14 applies to them where it reads: "*Wahev* ("friendship") in *Suphah* (a place-name)", and one shouldn't read here *Suphah*, but *sophah* ("at the end"). This means that fiercely differing opinions don't really matter, providing that after the discussion people go on living as friends in 'shalom'.

A passage elsewhere reads in the same spirit:[312] "Each dispute about the name of heaven, will still exist in the end, but a dispute not in the name of heaven will vanish in the end. What is a dispute in the name of heaven? That is the dispute between Shammai and Hillel.[b] And what is a dispute not in the name of heaven? That is the dispute of Korach and his group (Numbers 16)." There is another tradition about in-dept differences of opinion between the Schools of Sjammai and Hillel, which reads:[313] "Come and hear: even though the School of Shammai and the School of Hillel were divided *among themselves* about questions like: different wives, sisters, old bills of divorcements, doubts about the marriage of a wife, the case of a divorced woman who stayed the night in the same inn with her ex-husband [...], yet the School of Shammai continued marrying women from the School of Hillel and the School of Hillel continued marrying women from the School of Shammai, just to teach you that love and friendship reigned among them. Thus they fulfilled the verse from the Scripture: 'Love truth and peace' (Zechariah 8:19)."

---

a   See chapter 2, for the explanation of the play on words as well.

b   In the Talmud the opposite ideas of the Schools of Shammai and Hillel are frequently mentioned side by side without a distinct preference.

Maintaining peace among themselves is even so important that one, in doing so, can escape the punishment on idolatry, one of the worst offences in Judaism. Rabbi Eleazar said:[314] "Great is the peace, because even when Israel worships idols, but lives in peace with themselves and in one community with one another, the measure of justice won't hit them. After all it is said: 'Ephraim has attached himself to idols. Do not go near him!' (Hosea 4:17)." Here the word 'attached' is not only interpreted as 'attached to idols', but also as 'attached to each other'. As long as they are living in peace, God even endures their godlessness.

'Shalom' as a greeting[315]

The use of the word 'shalom' is already found in the Hebrew Bible and in the Apocrypha (Judges 6:23; 2 Kings 5:19; Tobit 12:17). In postbiblical Judaism the greeting 'shalom' is a very usual thing. Saying: 'shè'eilath shalom', one actually asks how someone is doing. The greeting is an expressions of politeness, and withholding it ranks as contempt or disdain. Who leaves this greeting unanswered behaves like a robber or a thief. This greeting and its correct reply runs usually: 'shalom alècha' ("peace for you") or 'shalom aleichem' (plural). In the rabbinical literature there are no indications that the ritual of greeting was bound by strict rules. But there had been discussions about the rules that should be applied when greeting someone during the prayer service.[316]

Greeting plays a part in some stories about rabbis. It's told about Rabban Jochanan ben Zakkai (1st century CE) that no one ever got the chance to greet him first, not even 'a pagan in the street', i.e. a stranger.[317] Rabbi Matthia ben Cheresh (ca. 130 CE) said:[318] "Approach everyone with the peace greeting. Be rather a tail with lions, than a head with foxes".[a] Just like Rabban Jochanan, Rabbi Marthia suppor-

---

a   There is an English proverb that runs: 'Better be the head of a dog than the tail of a lion', which means: 'better be a great servant than a small boss'. It seems to mean the contrary.

ted very much a peaceful coexistence with the Romans. Before the revolt of Bar Kochba (135 CE) he escaped from the land of Israel and settled in Rome.[319] In the language of the rabbis the lion and the fox are symbols of dedication to the Torah (the lion) and violation and neglect of the Torah (the fox).[320] So Rabbi Mathia's advice is that you'd better be the least among the followers of the Torah, than the strongest among the offenders of the Torah.

The use of the peace greeting wasn't restricted to Jews amongst themselves. For the sake of peace non-Jews are also greeted, even in a sabbatical year when they are working in the fields. But one isn't allowed to greet a Jew who works in the fields then, because he is committing an offence.[321] The medieval Jewish scholar Rashi even says about greeting pagans:[322] "One is allowed to greet the non-Israelites every day, although one imposes the name of God on them in doing so, for 'shalom' is a name of God" (see Judges 6:24). And Rabbi Tanchumah bar Abba (2nd half 4th century CE) said:[323] "When a non-Jew greets you with a good word (a blessing), answer with 'Amen'! After all it is said: 'You will be blessed by all nations' (Deuteronomy 7:14)." But one has to be careful during a non-Jewish festival. In that case one was only allowed to greet a non-Jew indistinctly in order not to give the impression that one supported him in his idolatry.[324]

Shalom in the services in Temple and synagogue

There are several indications that of old the sacrificial service was dominated by the idea of 'shalom' and that each reference to waging wars and carrying arms should be avoided in religious services in the Temple. In the instructions for the construction of the altar we read that iron objects are forbidden. After all, iron was the metal of war. The altar, as the place of atonement, should be constructed with "whole stones" (Deuteronomy 27:5-6). "Whole stones" are in Hebrew 'avanim shêleimoth', and this could also be translated with 'stones that will bring peace'.

Later on, when King David wants to build a temple for God in Jerusalem, he is forbidden to do so, because as a warlord he's shed to much blood (1 Chronicles 22:7-8). Only his son Solomon, the peaceful prince, was allowed to start building the Temple. A rabbinical commentary asks with regard to the construction of the Temple:[325] "Why do we read that Solomon counted strangers and appointed them as porters (see 2 Chron. 2:1, 16-17)? Why was such an important part in the construction of the Temple given to these strangers? To let you know that the Lord, blessed be He, brings nearer those who stand aloof [the strangers], and supports those who are far away, no less than those who are nearby. He rather gives 'shalom' to those who stand aloof [the strangers] than to those who are nearby [the Israelites]. As is said: 'Shalom, shalom, for those who are far away and those who are nearby[a] (Isaiah 57:19)."

In the rabbinical tradition the priestly office and 'shalom' are regularly interconnected. I already stated above that Aharon, the forefather of all priests, is seen as the prototype of all peace makers. Elsewhere a text from Malachi 2:6 is applied to Aharon:[326] "The Torah of truth was in his mouth, and injustice was not found on his lips. He walked with Me in peace (*shalom*) and equity, and turned many away from iniquity". Some sections before I mentioned the '*shalom*-covenant' (a treaty of welfare) between God and Aharon's grandson, the future high priest Phinehas (Numbers 25). Peace is strongly connected with serving God and the temple service is its pre-eminent example.[327] At the changing of the weekly priest service on sabbath the leaving guard said to the coming guard: "May He who does his Name live in this house, also cause to live among you love, affection, 'shalom' and friendship."[328]

The link between priesthood and 'shalom' emerges very pointedly indeed in the so called priestly blessing in Numbers 6:24-26. It's the blessing with which the priests blessed the people in the Temple in Jerusalem after the morning- and afternoon sacrifice. This blessing is still pronounced in the synagogue in the morning by the attendant priests, but only if there are ten adult Jews present (a socalled 'min-

---

a   Those who are far away, the strangers, are mentioned first.

jan'). This is – in Jewish legal sense – the necessary quorum for a congregation in stead of a collection of individuals. The rules for pronouncing the priestly blessing in the synagogue follow the ancient temple practice scrupolously. When not a priest but the cantor (*chazan*) recites this blessing, it is worded in a way that makes clear that here is someone speaking who's not a priest. In that case the priestly blessing proper has the character of a quotation:[329] "Our Lord and God of our fathers, bless us with the threefold blessing of the Torah, that is written by Moses, Your servant, that is said by Aharon and his sons, the priests, Your holy people, as is said: 'The Lord bless you and protect you, the Lord make his face to shine upon you and be gracious to you, the Lord lift up his countenance upon you and and give you *shalom*'." The whole ritual of the morning- and afternoon sacrifices ended via the priestly blessing in peace, in 'shalom'. In the rabbinical literature it is observed that also the description of the sacrifices in Leviticus 6 and 7 ends with the peace offering.[330] Reaching 'shalom' is the aim of the sacrificial service.

Peace is also one of the themes in all prayers in the synagogue. Rabbi Mani of She'av and Rabbi Jehoshu'ah of Sichnin said on behalf of Rabbi Levi:[331] "Great is the 'shalom', for all blessings, good and comfort, the Lord, blessed be He, brings to Israel, end in peace". As we saw in chapter 3, the same applies to the Standing- or Amidah-prayer (In Hebrew: *Shêmoneh Esreh*, i.e. the Eighteen Benedictions), which is the central prayer in the liturgy in the synagogue. The entire prayer ends in 'shalom' as its central theme. This last blessing is called in Hebrew 'Sim Shalom', after its first two words "grant peace":[332] "Grant *peace*, goodness, blessing, graciousness, kindness and compassion upon us and upon all of Your people Israel. Bless us, our Father, all of us as one, with the light of Your Face, for with the light of Your Face You have given us, Lord, our God, the Torah of life and a love of kindness, righteousness, blessing, mercy, life, and *peace*. And it may be good in Your eyes to bless your people Israel in every season and in every hour with Your *peace*. Blessed are you, Lord, Who blesses His people Israel with *peace*".

The six notions at the beginning of this blessing: peace, goodness, blessing, graciousness, kindness and compassion, are all found in the previous blessings of the Eighteen Benedictions (the Amidah-prayer), except the notion of 'peace' (shalom). This gives the blessing at the end of this prayer its specific character. The other five notions also refer just like 'peace' to the relation between God and man and between men together. Together they give meaning to the word the Shemoneh-Esreh-prayer ends in: "peace, wholeness, completeness", i.e. 'shalom'. As in the end the history of Israel and mankind will end in peace.[333] Four times does the word 'peace' appear in this last blessing, referring to the four corners of the earth. The 'shalom' is intended for the whole world in the end.

In the synagogue liturgy on sabbath, when the Shemoneh-Esreh-prayer is repeated, the priestly blessing is added by the cantor immediately before the *Sim-Shalom*-benediction. Some suppose that both blessing were recited in an alternating chant:[334]

Priestly blessing	Sim Shalom
Priests : The Lord bless you and protect you.	The people : Grant *peace*, goodness, blessing, graciousness, kindness and compassion upon us and upon all Israel, your people.
Priests : The Lord make his face to shine upon you and be gracious to you,	The people : Bless us, our Father, all of us as one, with the light of Your Face, for with the light of Your Face You have given us, Lord, our God: the Torah of life and a love of kindness, righteousness, blessing, mercy, life, and *peace*.
Priests : the Lord lift up his countenance upon you and give you 'shalom'."	The people : And it may be good in Your eyes to bless your people Israel in every season and in every hour with Your *peace*. Blessed are you, Lord, Who blesses His people Israel with *peace*".

This affinity between the priestly blessing and the Sim-Shalom-benediction is so large that *Sim Shalom* is called the 'priestly blessing' ('birkath kohanim') as well.[335]

Is peace the central point at the end of this Amidah-prayer, it is also at the beginning of the sabbath, the day of the world to come. The hymn 'Shalom aleichem' ("peace on you") is one of the songs that welcomes the sabbath on Friday evenings. Also the end of the 'Shêmah-Yisrael-prayer (the Hear-Israel -prayer) that is recited in the evening before one goes to bed, runs:[336] "Make us lay down Lord, our God, in peace and make us arise, our King, to life, and spread out above us the tent of your peace". So the day is concluded with thoughts of 'shalom'. And even the prayer remembering the dead, the Kaddish-prayer, ends with the call to 'shalom':[337] "May the fullness of peace and life fall to us and to all Israel from heaven. Say then: Amen. Who establishes peace on his hights, grant us and all Israel also peace. Say then: Amen."

The synagogue prayer service, of which, as shown in chapter 3, the most important function is to offer man the opportunity to reflect on what life's about[338], confronts the praying man repeatedly with 'shalom', not only as a condition to strive for, but more as a way of life man can make himself familiar with by praying.

Shalom and the messianic era

As seen in the preceding chapters, the partnership between God and man plays an essential part in the image of man in the Torah. Man's duty is to complete the world together with Him, because he's been created "in God's image" after all. It is exactly this thought of "being whole, complete, completion", that is the essence of the verb 'shalam', from which the word 'shalom' has been derived. Ultimately 'shalom' is the completion of the world on which God ànd man (ought to) work together.

In the idiom of the Hebrew Bible and in the later Jewish tradition 'shalom' is often described as a gift from God to mankind (Psalm 29:11; Isaiah 26:12; 45:7). However, this doesn't mean that there will be 'shalom' without man's cooperation. After all, a central point in Hebrew thought is that man should participate in God's creation, it is even stated that God won't be able to reach His aim with the creation without man's cooperation.[a, 339] When, at a meal, God is blessed because of the "bread he brings forth from the earth", one is only allowed to say these words when there is real bread on the table. What in this blessing is ascribed to God however, is achieved by man through unremitting labour. To make bread he must plough, sow, mow, thresh, mill, knead and bake, not to mention transporting all these materials. As with bread, it is with 'shalom'. Before God can grant 'shalom', people should have entered into mutual relations, should have made arrangements to safeguard these relations, should have restored them after any disruptions, etc. In the Torah, the Holy One, blessed be He, has given directions how to reach this 'shalom': by living fair and amicably with each other. If and when Israel enters into this covenant of the Torah, the Lord will grant them 'shalom', according to the obligations of his 'covenant of peace' (Numbers 25:12).

The prophets interpreted the history of Israel from this relation between covenant and 'shalom'. If the people keep the arrangements of the covenant, they'll enjoy 'shalom'. However, if they break the covenant, God will take away his blessing of the people. Should the people return to the Lord, there will be 'shalom' again. Already in the 26th chapter of Leviticus – see verse 6 for the word 'shalom' – the foundation is laid for this relation. The exile is often seen by the prophets and later by the rabbis as well, as punishment for – or better: as an intrinsic consequence of – the refusal of the then generations to fulfil their obligations. But even in the exile the possibility remains that the 'shalom' will be restored in the future (Isaiah 32:17-18; Ezekiel 34:25). Always, in dead-end situations new leaders will rise again, men like Moses, Joshua and David, to help to find again 'shalom' and to help to bring nearer the final aim of creation.[b, 340]

---

a   This goes for the creation of the Hebrew Bible as 'Word of God' as well.
b   See e.g. Deuteronomy 18:15ff; Isaiah 9:6-7; Zechariah 9:9-10; Psalm 72:7.
    Prudence is called for when trying to link up these texts with the coming of

In post-biblical Judaism the notion of future leaders who help bringing nearer the 'shalom' of the world to come is connected with the idea of the 'mashi'ach' (messiah), the anointed one of the Lord, who will help his people to liberate themselves from the subjection by other nations. The basic assumption of rabbinical thought is not so much the messiah as a person, but rather the aim of his actions, the establishment of the messianic era. This messianic era will be an era of peace, and the rabbinical tradition expresses this in many places, for instance with the words: "There is no greater good in the world than peace [for it is said]: 'because the last, the future of man, will be peace' (Psalm 37:37)."[341, a] In another tradition Rabbi José the Galilean says:[342] "Great is the peace, for when the messianic king will manifest himself to Israel, he will just begin with peace. After all, it is said: 'How delightful is it to see approaching over the mountains the feet of a messenger who announces peace, a messenger who brings good news, who announces deliverance" (Isaiah 52:7). The name of the messiah is also 'peace', because it also reads: "Everlasting father, prince of peace" (Isaiah 9:6).

The image of man is – as already stated – closely linked up with 'shalom'and the world to come – the messianic era – in which God and man as partners work together at the perfection, the 'shalom' of the world. As shown in the previous section the Jewish prayer service which confronts man continuously with his part in the world, is also aimed at reaching the 'shalom', the peace, the completion of the world. The rabbinical tradition about the world to come, the messianic era, and the synagogue prayers are in line with the perspective the prophets outlined of a time of everlasting peace.

Peace also played a constant part in the reflections of the later Jewish scholars. For instance, they asked themselves how to imagine that

a later messiah, as these texts don't speak about an 'anointed one of the Lord' (see endnote).
a   The translation of Psalm 37:37 is in this tradition the literary rendering of the Hebrew text: "for [the] end of [that] man [will be] peace". (NKJV: 'For the future of [that] man [is] peace).

final 'shalom' for all people and all nations? Certainly not as an era with all opposites having disappeared off the face of the earth. The 15th century Spanish-Jewish philosopher Josef Albo defines 'shalom' as the harmony of opposites. The one won't dominate the other anymore. According to this definition 'peace' doesn't mean the removal of all differences that exist between God and man and between man and his neighbour. According to him peace is an ideal order, a coming to fullness or a full combination of opposites,[343] and the heaven can serve as an example. The Hasidic Rabbi Pinchas of Koretz said:[344] "The heavens (*sjamajim*) came into being because God made '*shalom*' between fire (*eish*) and water (*majim*).[a] Who, in doing so, brought the extreme opposites to 'shalom' with each other, will also bring us all to 'shalom' with each other." So after having reached the final 'shalom' there will be a fascinating world.

There is probably no other religion in which peace and well-being play such important parts as in Judaism. And there is probably no other book than the Hebrew Bible in which peace and well-being are so much interwoven. Peace in the sense of 'shalom' is more than the absense of war, violence and aggression. It's, in the end, the condition of welfare and well-being for all nations of the world, the condition the creation is destined for. The great 'shalom' the world is heading for, is the completion of the creation in which God and man work together. The image of man in the Torah inspires us up till now to find that way en work on it.

---

a   This thought fits in with a possible composition of the word sjamajim ('heavens') from the words eish ('fire') and majim ('waters'), though this is etymologically uncertain.

6 The Torah and other Images of Man

In the preceding chapters I discussed a number of aspects of the image of man in the Torah. The gist of it is this: God created man as his partner in the creative process. God and man entered into several pacts and during this process the duties and rights of these treaties developed more and more into the direction of its climax: the Torah Moses received at the Sinai. It is imperative to man that he studies the Torah, that he examines, discusses, explains, elaborates and uses it in actual life. His is the responsibility to restore any disturbed relation with man or God, after any misbehaviour. Prayer is a means to stay permanently conscious of his task and to keep reflecting on it. Man is expected to contribute to the organization of a just society, to perform acts of friendship for his fellow men and to work on peace and welfare of the entire mankind, without regard to his fellow man's faith or agnosticism.

Though the reader will be able to connect much of the material discussed in previous chapters with matters that today will come up in the social and religious debates as well, it may be important – in order to obtain a better understanding of the special character of the image of man in the Torah – to investigate more closely its position in relation to other existing images of man. Inevitably, such an investigation will be limited here, as for the size and the depth, because the planning of this book doesn't allow for another four or five extra chapters. Therefore I'll deal briefly with some current images of man, which play an important part in our society today. The images of man of Christianity and Islam certainly belong to this, but also the images that often play a decisive part in the background, in science and secular society, in discussions and in definitions of one's position.

This chapter, however, doesn't deal with those images of man as they are only. It is especially important for the purpose of this book to compare those images regularly with the image of man in the Torah. Next to the parallels, I'll especially stress the differences with the image of man in the Torah. After all, these differences show best the special positions from which man's thought develop. Insight into the differences between these images can turn – in my firm belief – the social and religious debate from a dialogue between deaf people into a dialogue between listeners.

The image of man in Christianity[345]

Why does, in this book about the image of man in the Torah, this section bear the title *The image of man in Christianity* instead of *The image of man in the New Testament,* or *The image of man in the Gospels*? This has everything to do with my own position within Christianity, as I explained in earlier publications.[a] In them I argued that the Gospels, if not the entire New Testament, consist of Jewish writings, showing a great affinity with the then Pharisaic-rabbinic Judaism, from which today's Judaism has developed. Read from that point of view I can find few or no differences between the image of man of the Gospels and the image of man of the Torah, as expounded in the previous chapters. And yet the image of man in Christianity differs completely with the image of man in the Torah. This difference has everything to do with the development the awakening Christianity experienced from the 2nd century CE under the influence of Graeco-Roman thought, a development that caused it to alienate from Judaism.

The image of man in orthodox Christianity is of post biblical origine. It was formed from halfway the 2nd century CE by the Christian apologetes and the later Greek and Latin churchfathers, educated, every one of them, in the Graeco-Roman schools.[346] The consequence has been that in Christianity human life and the relation between God and man have been understood quite differently for ages than is the case in the Jewish tradition. The image of man in orthodox Christianity, that still makes itself strongly felt in modern-Christian ideas though, consists of two opposite essential characteristics. On the one hand man is seen as a creature of God and thus as his *image bearer*. This side of man

---

a   For a summary of my earlier work see the website www.petervantriet.nl.

shows what God meant him to be as a free being that loves God and his fellow men and does the right thing. In the description of this side of man notions like 'love' and 'freedom' play an important part.[347] On the other hand man is seen as a *sinner*. This wicked* side of man refers to what *he himself has made of it*. In some dissertations about this side of the image of man notions like 'misery'[348], 'guilt' and 'fate' occupy an important place.[349] Sin, guilt, error, inadequacy, helplessness, misery, mortality and the like, are notions that for orthodox Christians are inextricably and fundamentally bound up with man's excistence, even to the extent that these aspects dominate his *natural* existence completely as far as it takes place outside the redemption in Christ. It is, then, this second, dark side of man's life that is discussed extensively in dogmatic literature.[350]

If we compare the orthodox Christian image of man with the image of man of the Torah, it's especially the interpretation of the notion of sin and its consequence for man's religious life that deserves the attention. For instance in dogmatic literature, sin is described as 'an abuse of freedom', 'a senseless and perilous rebellion against God'.[351] The point is that in the first place it's not about actual acts that go against God's will, but about a basic characteristic of man's existence. Man *does* not only *sin*, he *is* a *sinner* especially. According to the orthodox Christian conviction sin is first and foremost a wicked attitude to life, a wrong existence,[352] or "a profound unwillingness towards God, that preceeds one's actions and that works through them".[353] Being a sinner lies rooted in being human, it's not influenced by personal decisions, it's "destined".[354]

The words used to describe sin, make one think sometimes of a deadly, contagious disease. The Dutch Roman Catholic New Catechism (1966) talks about:[355] "degrees of being contagious of our sins"; "sins that affect every man"; "contagion by the sins of others". Since the churchfather Augustine (354-430 CE) the belief exists that one gets sin already at one's birth. This "original sin" (*peccatum originale*) is an inheritance of one's parents.[356] So sin isn't anything *to* man, it's an all-embracing qualification of his existence.[357] It lies deeply embedded in man's heart[358] and it goes through man's whole life as a sphere that cannot be located.[359]

In dogmatic literature this negative side of man's existence is painted in garish colours. If we want to describe man's condition we stumble upon expressions like: "a deep, mysterious guiltiness", "a vast, ineluctable, concerted, but yet guilty impotence to love"[360]; "a life in guilt, growing into depravation and ending in utter godforsakenness"; "an apple, rotten inside"; "a condition of being completely lost".[361] And of wide repute are the words of the Heidelberg Catechism: "Sunday 3 Question 8: Are we then so corrupt that we are wholly incapable of doing any good, and inclined to all wickedness? Answer: Yes, we, etc."[362] We also come upon radical wordings for the disturbed relation of man towards God. Man is revealed by God as being: "lost sons, rebels against the order of his holy love, enemies of his realm". In Jesus man is confronted with his radical and total estrangement from God.[363]

For one thing, sin has a collective aspect in the orthodox Christian point of view, valid for mankind as a whole, and there is the individual aspect for the other.[364] Sin is for many orthodox Christians a dominant characteristic of man's existence. After all, God created mankind and the world excellently, but by breaking the rules of God's law man has dragged down himself and the creation into a state of moral imperfection and religious depravation, which permeate one's whole life and the whole society. The true cause of sin is found in "wilful disobedience" or in "the evil desire of a free being".[365] Man always uses his freedom to turn away from God and his intentions with mankind.[366] Sin is not only man's radical estrangement from God, but man is also powerless to struggle out of that situation. According to the churchfather Augustine (354-430 CE) and the church reformer Martin Luther (1483-1546) man lost his freedom because of sin and has no longer a free, but a servile will, so he simply *can't* back out of it.[367]

However, it should be said that all kinds of mutual differences exist among orthodox Christians in the way they look at the two sides of being human and especially the wicked side of it.[368] For instance, the

Eastern Churches[a] consider sin a degeneration of the originally perfect existence of man. Their attention is especially turned to questions of mortallity, reincarnation, ressurrection and the like. Western Christians[b] in particular consider sin as disturbing the relation with God. They very much emphasize matters like guilt, justification, mercy and the like. And within Western Christianity there are differences in nuance as well. The Roman-Catholic doctrine stresses with regard to the notion of "sin", more the factuality of specific acts of man, whereas the Reformation rather accentuates the fact that man is a sinner entirely,[369] though it should be said it's not an absolute contrast in all respects.

In orthodox Christianity it's only thanks to God, that the troubled relation between God and man has been restored in principle. He has done so by making his son Jesus Christ suffer the imperfect human existence till death, and next by delivering him from it. Central in this is the so-called means of atonement of Christ's suffering and death on the cross and his resurrection. In this way mankind gets a view of salvation and a better existence. Man as an individual can get remission of his guilt, on the condition that he acknowledges his sinful and imperfect existence, and faithfully accepts Christ's work of salvation and reconciliation. This event of salvation transcends in its meaning very much its actual historic form and is seen, for that matter, as an act of salvation by God exclusively. So it should be possible to speak about a historic-transcendent event of salvation, that goes far beyond place, time and circumstances that characterize it historically. As far as people will be involved in this proces, they will play, of course, a completely minor part.

As a subordinate question there is also the believer's own involvement in the event of salvation. Even for his faithful acceptance of Christ, his own activity is, in the eyes of many Christians, inadequate. In man's life two opposite tendencies come up. The first tendency, the one towards death, springs from the heart of human existence, the

---

a   Eastern-, Greek- and Russian-orthodox Christians.
b   The Roman-Catholic and Protestant Christians.

totally disrupted relation to God. The other tendency, the one towards keeping life, springs from God's beneficial plan with man.[370] In this view man can only come to faith because God himself will let him be born again through the Holy Spirit.[371] Only when and if one has become a born-again man, the relation with God should play again a part of some meaning by trying to live a Christian life. There is less unanimity about this Christian life than about the Christian doctrine. Sometimes it is indicated as the imitation of Christ *(imitatio christi)*. In that case simplicity, repentance and austerity are stressed. It can mean a monastic life with a lot of stress on prayers or even more on willingness to help. Attending services, saying prayers and doing good, or – in the protestant tradition – works of gratitude, are certainly part of it. But all these contributions to the realm of God are insignificant compared with Christ's work of salvation.

In a nutshell: the relation between God and man in orthodox Christianity boils down to this:

- Man has been created perfectly, but disrupted himself by sin and is therefore totally responsible for the disruption of his relation towards God;
- This disruption has caused an absolute contrast between God's perfection and man's wickedness;
- The restoration of this relation by the sacrificial death and resurrection of Jesus Christ is solely God's work, to which humans have not been able to contribute, essentially;
- Only when and after man will have accepted this mediation of Christ, he will be able to go and play a part of some meaning in his relation towards God, but even then this relation will be via Christ as mediator;
- One is suppused to lead a Christian life as citizen of God's realm.

In modern Christian theology however, man's part in the relation towards God is by and large bigger and more independent than in the orthodox religious doctrine. Via new developments in the study of the Old Testament the contemporary theology is greatly influenced by the image of man in the Torah. Because of this, matters like sin, error and guilt are no longer so heavily emphasized. But the above sketched pattern of the orthodox Christianity reproduces the basic characteristics of a Christian faith as has been adhered to by the vast majority of Christians for ages and is still professed in a lot of churches. This appears, for instance, from the first declaration with a dogmatic character about the meaning of Jesus, drawn up by the combined synods of the three Protestant Churches in the Netherlands in 2000, churches which merged into the Protestant Church of the Netherlands four years later. In this declaration Jesus is described as the Son of God who has freed man from his guilt by his death on the cross.[372] And the Roman-Catholic liturgy still makes the participants in the Eucharist say: "Lord, I am not worthy to receive you, but only say the word and I shall be healed".[a] One can't say this in a covenant of partners. But even the works of modern theologians are still very much influenced by the old dogmatic outlines of the orthodox Christian image of man.[373]

When we compare the orthodox Christian image of man with the image of man in the Torah, the most important difference that attracts our attention is that the element of partnership between God and man is absent. In the orthodox Christian point of view man doesn't play an essential part in the perfection of the creation. On the contrary, God should deliver him from his lost state by the mediation of His Son Jesus Christ. This important difference is followed by all kinds of other differences some of which I already mentioned briefly in the previous chapters.

For instance, the idea that man should work on his own perfection by means of a learning process, doesn't play any part in Christianity. On the contrary, man should *let* himself be delivered. Study and knowledge are not assignments for every believer. For ages this has been the clergy's field. For laymen it'll be enough to learn the outlines of the Christian faith during a limited period of catechism when adults

---

a   Here the word of a centurion for the benefit of his sick servant in Matthew 8:8 is generalised and made into an essential feature of man. See also: http://americamagazine.org/content/all-things/my-soul-shall-be-healed.

– young or old – are being prepared for baptism or confession of faith.[a] Prayer also has – save perhaps praise and grace – in the orthodox Christianity another function than is the case in the image of man in the Torah. The aspect of meditation and introspection to support man's assignment to help to perfect life and the world, is completely absent in orthodox Christian prayers. Here prayer veers into the direction of asking for divine benevolence, remission of sins and intervention for the sake of the welfare of the faithful and of the world.[b] Also justice and mercy is looked at differently. In orthodox Christianity mercy and charity are not a right but a favour for the destitute. And finally for orthodox Christians the coming of the Messianic reign is not something they can help bringing about. Only God can establish his realm on earth at the end of time.

Christianity – as I stated earlier – evolved from the first-century Judaisme as an outright Jewish movement when the books of the New Testament were created. That's why reflection on the image of man in the Torah, could bring modern Christians into contact again with their religion as it once had begun and as it was meant to be. From this point of view today's dialogue between Christians and Jews could – perhaps – get new dynamics.

The Image of Man in the Koran

Today a book like this which pays attention – albeit in brief – to the most important images of man which influenced our Western culture, ought to pay some attention to the Islam as well. Since the sixties of last century large numbers of Muslims have settled in Europe and America. Due to the big, cultural difference between the west and the eastern countries they or their ancestors come from, numerous problematical situations arise in our society, that ask for solutions by the

---

a   Dependent on what kind of baptism one practises: baptism of adults or baptism of children.

b   In intercessory prayer for instance, God is repeatedly beseeched to have mercy on all kinds of abuse in the world.

authorities, by social organizations (among them the Churches) and by individual citizens. Maybe a comparison of the image of man in de Koran, the holy book of the Muslims, with the image of man in the Torah, will be able to enlighten the understanding of the intercultural problems we experience together. An investigation like that will – hopefully – contribute to define one's position clearly in the public debate.

Studying the Islam as a non-Muslim means that we have to be careful not to be too easily charmed by the many similarities with Judaism and Christianity. Those similarities are indeed big, but we should recognize that the differences are deep and fundamental, which is certainly the meaning of the Muslims themselves. After all, the Koran is seen by them as the final and definitive revelation of Allah.[a] It's true, Allah revealed himself also to Jews and Christians in times past. For instance, *Musa* (Moses) was given the *Tawrah* (Torah) and *Isa* (Jesus) the *Injil* (the Gospels). Of course, they were major prophets and originally their books contained the pure revelations from the primeval book that was with Allah. But yet the pure revelation of the Koran was needed because these earlier revelations were only directed to a specific people and because they were corrupted and falsified by Jews and Christians alike.[374]

Many Muslims feel, with regard to their own religion, very superior and they not only direct this feeling to themselves but also to mankind as a whole. They consider the revelations of the Koran with regard to Allah's indivisible unity and singularity as unique for the Islam. This faith is to their firm belief the Islam's revolutionary contribution to the history of man.[375, b] Those who believe in this unity of Allah are expected to be *one* community. If that is the case and if the com-

---

a I avoided to translate Allah with "God", nowadays often used by many Christian authors, because I am of the opinion that in our field of language the word "God" evokes other associations than needed to understand the Islamic concept of God.

b Ignoring the fact that Judaism already formulated the indivisible unity and singularity of God in the Torah (Deuteronomy 6:4) at least a millennium earlier, and still professes it consistently today.

munity of believers keeps the rules of conduct of the Islam, then it'll be the best community possible among men.[376] Human knowledge of Allah and His characteristics is only possible thanks to Allah's self-revelation in the Koran.[377] Moreover, Muslims assume that every child is born in a "state of *islam*", i.e. submission to Allah, and so is a *Muslim* by nature. And it is in this sense that the Islam is seen as the natural religion of all people.[378] It's true, Judaism and Christianity are tolerated religions for the Koran, but in an islamic society they have a status of a tolerated minority with limited rights and special obligations.[379]

So Islam understands itself as the ultimate religion for all people, Jews and Christians alike, and this attitude evokes a problem for the interreligious dialogue. The Jews too, take the superiority of their own religion for granted, but they only see it as an assignment to themselves, not to the rest of mankind. For centuries Christians had the same idea about the superiority of *their* religion like the Muslims, but after the Holocaust and under the influence of the oecumenic movement, many of them have at least learnt and accepted Judaism as a legitimate road to God. Therefore Jews and Christians should continue to ask Muslims about the consequences of their self-understanding for coexistence, not only in the West, but especially also in those parts of the world that are traditionally Islamic. In order to be able to have an interreligious dialogue it is important to have a good perception of the image of man in the Koran.

A dominant characteristic of the image of man in the Koran is that Allah created man as a servant (Sura 51:56).[a, 380] The same is true of all other beings in the heavens and upon the earth (Sura 19:93). The Koran denies explicitly that Allah would have adopted a son (Sura 19:92). The image of God as a father for His children, so important in the Hebrew Bible and the New Testament, is not found in the Koran for Allah. But man does appear to be someone who doesn't obey Allah (Sura 80:23).[381] So the relation between Allah and man is seen as a relation between a Lord and his rebellious servant.[382]

---

a   Representing the verses I'll follow the eastern version as rendered in the Dutch Koran-translation of Kramers (1974).

In line with this relation between Allah and man as "Lord and servant", the relation between man and woman is defined differently in the Koran than in the Torah. Allah created man from *one* soul and from this his wife, "so that he could find his rest with her" (Sura 7:189).[383] Nevertheless both are rewarded equally for the good and punished for the evil they do,[384] but man is superior to woman, because Allah prefers men: a woman should obey her husband and if not she should be disciplined (Sura4:34).[385] And in spite of the fact that Mohammed treated his wives excellently,[386] a woman in the Koran is submitted to her husband and should serve him. This is not the case in the Torah. It speaks about equality first: "male and female He created them" (Genesis 1:27) and next about partnership: a woman is for a man "a helper opposed to him"(Genesis 2:18).[a, 387]

According to the Koran, man – after his creation – remained initially in paradise, situated in heaven. Allah created man well, good of nature, good of mind. But the Satan, stirring up trouble all the time among the servants of Allah, manages to bring down man by seducing man's proud and arrogant ego to rebel against the Creator.[388] Nevertheless, man himself is responsible for his iniquities. His punishment is banishment to the earth down there. Only after the resurrection from death, there is the possibility to return to paradise (Sura 7:19-25).[389] So human existence is seen as a transitional stage on the road back to paradise. Again, the contrast with the image of man in the Torah is big here: in the Torah man is created on the earth with the assignment to work and to keep the earthly paradise (Genesis 2:15).

From the moment man – after his expulsion from paradise – dwells on the earth, his moral situation is full of danger, according to the Koran. Indeed, the Koran doesn't recognize the existential wickedness so characteristic in orthodox Christianity, but man's responsibility for the evil in the world is big. That's because Allah entered into a covenant with mankind even before He had created man. According to this covenant He has accepted the obligation to reveal himself to man via

---

a   See Rashi's commentary here. Martin Buber and Franz Rosenzweig translate: "a help(er) facing him" (see endnote).

prophets and messengers. This covenant is two-sided for man: Allah's revelation is not only a source of salvation through faith and obedience to His will, but also a standard to condemnation and punishment of those who refuse to obey Him and to believe in Him.[390] The Koran talks about following one's own inclinations and desires as the cause of the deviation. Facing desire and wicked inclination is "know-ledge" as revealed in the Koran.[391] So man is responsible for all evil whereas all good comes from Allah (Sura 4:79).[392] It is underlined repeatedly in the Koran that Allah doesn't wrong anyone, but that people wrong themselves.[393]

In this respect the Koran knows a strong dualism of behaviour. Man is constantly confronted with the choice between good and bad behavior. The moral imperative of the Islam is often represented with the words: "(One should) command the decent, forbid the reprehensible and believe in Allah."[394] The two notions ma'ruf ("known, familiar, social acceptabel") and munkar ("unknown, strange") expresses what has been commanded and forbidden. A second set of notions that plays a part in this, is haram ("forbidden") and halal ("allowed"). Again and again the Koran stresses the fact that one should prescribe and follow what is correct and forbid what is wrong.[395]

In various places the Koran further defines the good Allah tells people to do: generosity and charity; buying the slaves' freedom; giving food to the poor; treating well one's parents; not squandering the orphans' possessions; not drinking wine; not taking part in gambling; not asking interest (usury); etc. The incentive to do well is very often accompanied by the promise of the reward for this good behaviour on the Last Judgement. But also the punishment that can be expected is the prospect of someone who does evil and refrains from doing well. "You will be answerable," are words that often return (e.g. in Sura 17:34 and 36).[396] And: "Allah watches your doings closely" (Sura 2:265).

The reward of paradise and punishment with the fire of hell are often described as something that can be expected in future, not only in the Koran, but also in the hadith, the authoritative tradition. A characteristic saying of Mohammed in the hadith is:[397] "You should be true, because the truth leads to virtue and virtue leads to paradise. You should not lie, because the lie leads to sin and sin to the fires of hell." Even the invocation of the Koran, prayed daily a number of times by pious Muslims, is pervaded with this dualism of behaviour: "In the name of Allah, the Merciful. Praise to Allah, the Lord of the Worlds, the Merciful, the Ruler on Judgement Day. You we serve and ask for help. Lead us unto the right path, the path of those to whom you grant your favours, on whom there is no wrath and who not go astray."[398]

This dualism of behaviour is strongly linked with the belief in the last day, the Day of Judgement. On this day all dead will arise and all people will have to account for their actions and belief. Who is judged favourably in this judgement awaits paradise, who is found guilty awaits the fires of hell. This point of faith stresses very much man's individual responsibility and freedom of choice, and is consequently the pre-eminent incentive that supports the ethical imperative of Islam.[399]

However, to be sure that one will be judged favourably in the Last Judgement, one must become and be a faithful Muslim. The literal meaning of the word *islam* is 'submission' and a Muslim is someone who is in the state of *islam*, the state of submission. In the Koran man is frequently incited to submit to Allah[400] and, in doing so, to become a servant of Allah (Arabic: *abd allah*). *Islam* is also described as the total submission to the will of Allah. This will grant him or her: inner peace, an honourable character in this life and protection against divine revenge in the life to come.[401]

The submission to Allah is as the submission to one's lord and master and so the Muslim knows and believes to be completely dependent of Him.[402] This religious attitude of submission to Allah fits in with the relation of master and servant being characteristic for the image of man in the Koran, as already mentioned above.] It differs quite clearly with the image of man in the Torah, which is specifically characterized by a *partnership* between God and man. Nowhere in the Torah the term 'servant' or 'slave' (Hebrew *èved*) is used to characterize the relation between God and man generally, not even for the relation between God and the Israelites especially.[403] On the other hand, the word 'servant' concerns the Israelites' bondage in Egypt (e.g. in Deuteronomy 24:18), and it is exactly this bondage God helped them to escape from. And next only persons with a special status like Moses are called 'servant of the Lord' with regard to his special assignment as leader of Israel (e.g. in Exodus 4:20).[404] The verb 'to serve' concerns the temple service particularly. Being a servant is in the Torah not the essence of being man, but a characteristic only of people in special circumstances. This important difference between the images of man in Torah and Koran is also found again in the meaning of the words *mosque* and *synagogue (beit haknesset)*: for 'synagogue' means 'place of gathering (of free people)', and the word 'mosque' means 'place of bowing down (as a servant or slave)'.[a, 405]

The Islam claims – just like orthodox Christianity – to be the only true religion (Sura 9:33). Who desires to adhere to another religion, will in future (on Judgement Day) be part of the lost ones (Sura 3:85). The submission to Allah is, in addition to the word *islam*, more often indicated with the word 'faith' or 'belief', meaning specifically that one listens to Him, follows His words and obeys Him. This obedience appears especially from doing deeds as required from the Muslim in the Koran. In doing so, obedience to Allah and obedience to Mohammed merge into each other: 'Who obeys the messenger, obeys Allah' (Sura 4:80).[406]

The conversion to the Islam should happen of one's own free will. Mohammed can call on people to it, but he's unable to bring them to conversion, let alone his followers should be able to do this. It's Mohammed's task to warn, to remind, to preach. The thought of pressure for conversion is rejected: "And when your Lord [= Allah] should have wanted this, all those in the world should have believed. How then should you force people to come to the faith?" (Sura 10:99).[407] On the other hand the infidel awaits the fires of hell on Judgement Day

---

a   The English word for mosque has been derived – via the Spanish mesquita – from the Arabic word masdjid, i.e. the place where one bows down (see endnote).

(Sura 5:10), since "those who die not believing, for them we [= Allah] prepared painful punishment" (Sura 4:18).[408]

Worse however, than remaining not conversed, is the turning away from those who'd acceded, like the hypocrites who had kept up the appearance of being islamic.[409] They deserve death (Sura 4:89). There is no way back to Islam for apostates (Sura 3:90). The *sharia*, the Islamic law, states the death penalty for apostasy and even important Islamic scholars have not yet distanced themselves from this up to now.[410, a]

Next submission (*islam*) demands one to agree with certain points of faith and to obey certain rules of behaviour. Islam is both a doctrine and practice of life. It rests on the five so-called pillars: reciting the creed, praying the ritual prayer (*salat*), paying the religious taxt (*zakat*), fasting in the month of *ramadan* and pilgrimage to Mekka *(hajj)*. All but the first of these 'pillars' belong to the *sharia*, the Islamic law. And by reciting the creed one puts oneself also under the *sharia*.[411] The doctrine, in its turn, consists of five, and according to some, of six points:[412]

1. *The belief in the existence of Allah and His indivisible unity and singularity* – This should not be doubted.
2. *The existence of angels* – They are in the transcendent world with Allah and function as the links between Allah and mankind.
3. *The belief in the mission of messengers and prophets* – From Adam till the last prophet Mohammed, Allah made His revelations known via them.
4. *The belief in the revealed scriptures* – As the last revealed Scripture the Koran is eternal, the firm foundation of everything. It's Allah's uncreated word.[413]
5. *The belief in the Day of Judgement* – On this day all the dead will rise and all people will have to give account, personally, of their faith

---

a   The Torah knows capital punishment as well (e.g. in Numbers 25:1-5), but in the days of the rabbis it was no longer executed. The New Testament though, knows this punishment also, for deceiving the congregation (Acts 5:1-6).

and good deeds. Who, in this judgement, is judged favourably awaits paradise, who is condemned awaits the fires of hell (Sura 18:103-108).[414] This point of doctrine emphasizes greatly the individual responsibility and freedom of choice of man on the one hand. But the called up fear for the hell imposes a lot psychological pressure on people, to make them follow the Koran's rules.

6. *The belief in Allah's decrees* – The doctrine of predestination (Arabic: *qadar*): is connected to this point of faith: At the creation already Allah had decreed who among mankind should walk the way of virtue and who should walk the way of evil.[a, 415] This image of god in the Koran does not only turn up with non-Muslims but also with many Muslims themselves.[416]

Even if one is Muslim, watchfulness is called for. The general message is that people must give account of their actions to their Creator after this earthly life.[417] The Koran frequently calls on man to ask Allah for forgiveness. Those who do so, will indeed be granted forgiveness and should not despair. After all, Allah is described repeatedly as merciful, benevolent, the Forgiving One.[418] Time and again the Koran verses end in the phrase 'Allah is forgiving' or 'Allah is ready to forgive'. "Those who turn back full of remorse and do good deeds, for them Allah will change their evil deeds into good ones. Allah is forgiving and merciful" (Sura 25:70).[419] The Koran is considered the eternal guideline and recovery for the Muslims, recovery from their wrongdoings.[420] Allah's mercy expresses itself especially in the remission of sins. The Koran speaks about this countless times. The condition, however, is that one should listen to the words of Mohammed: "Oh, our people, reply to Allah's herald and believe in Allah, then He will forgive your sins and keep you from grievous punishment" (Sura 46:30). "See, verily, I [= Allah] am forgiving towards him who reforms and becomes pious and allows himself to be led" (Sura 20:82).

---

a   This issue is at odds with the previous point and in the Islamic dogmatic literature one therefore tries to harmonize both issues (See also the endnote).

In many places the Koran concerns itself very dualistically with the opposition between good and evil, reward and punishment, paradise and hell. This now, is found – in this way – neither in the Torah, nor in the New Testament. Indeed, in these Scriptures many parts deal with acting well or badly, and reward and punishment is spoken about, but a permanent threat of punishment in case one acts badly, is out of the question. This indeed should not befit a relation between God and man which is after all a partnership. The big and constant emphasis of the Koran on Allah's mercy, is understandable considering the fact that He is a strict Lord for His submissive servants, servants who can ignore His will at any moment and who can provoke His anger. But in the Torah the Lord is rather a father with grown-up children. They study together with Him as a Teacher, they argue with Him and "wrestle" to reach a more and more well-defined insight how to behave. And in case they arouse His anger, it's about extreme situations. In the Torah His forgiveness is not constantly stressed and not under discussion, and the thought of hell isn't found in the Torah at all.[a]

Also the idea of covenants in the Koran (see above) differs from that in the Torah. In the Koran the covenant between Allah and man was already made even before man was created. This now is not possible in the image of man in the Torah. The covenant or partnership of God is a covenant with men of flesh and blood, and living in real, historical situations. This is connected with the belief that the notion of "peace" is another one. The idea of *shalom*, peace and well-being for all people, which should be worked on to complete the creation of the world, doesn't play a part in the Koran. The Arabic word for 'peace', *salam*, is of the same root as the word *islam*, which – as we saw – means submission. When the Koran speaks of peace, it is in terms of conque-

---

a   The later Jewish tradition does recognize the idea of a "hell" or gêhinnom (see e.g. the story about Rabbi Akiva and Tinneius Rufus in chapter 4), but this idea only plays a minor part in the stories and reflections.

ring the unbelievers (Sura 4:90-91; 47:35).[a, 421] The state of real peace has been reached when the power is in the hands of the Moslims (Sura 4:91). Islamic law doesn't recognize the possibility of a peaceful relation with 'unbelievers and unfaithful', even though a long-term armistice – as long as the other one can't be submitted – belongs to the possibilities. In Islamic theology the non-Islamic part of the world is known as the "war zone".[422]

Finally some remarks on the character of the Koran as a religious book, because that differs very much as well with the Torah. The Torah being especially a textbook for each individual believer even if read in public, the Koran is a book mainly to be read aloud in public. The word *Koran* means literally "recitation",[423] i.e. that which is recited on behalf of Allah. The Koran came into being in that way: the words were put by or on behalf of Allah into Mohammed's heart[424] and then he recited them literally, after which his followers wrote them down literally. That, at least, is the traditional Islamic view on the origin of the book.

Therefore, the text of the Koran must be learned by heart and be recited by rote during prayer, this in contrast with the Torah, which should be read from the scroll during the service.[425] Even though understanding the text is important so that it can be used as a guiding principle for life,[426] the function of the Koran is not so much being a textbook that must be studied, worked out further and completed, such as the Torah, but being a well-rounded diktat of Allah to the people. In addition the Torah recognizes a continuing revelation which will perform in due course (Deuteronomy 18:18). The Koran however, doesn't know this. According to its own statement, the Koran is the explanation of everything (Sura 12:11), makes everything clear (Sura 44:3), and overlooks nothing (Sura 6:38).[427] After Mohammed there won't be any new prophets.

---

a   The word "peace" doesn't happens superfluous in the Koran and
    especially in the sense of ending or preventing a war (see endnote). In the
    translations the word "peace" is often used to render a "mutual
    agreement" (e.g. Sura 2:224).

Without any doubt the Islam should be considered an improvement compared to the polytheistic Arabic culture in earlier times. Mohammed introduced improvements on many points: the organization of the society on the basis of justice and mercy; the abolition of interest (usury), which kept the poor poor;[428] the position of woman by curtailment of polygamy and better rules for divorce;[429] curtailment of blood feud;[430] and so on. He adopted a lot from Judaism and the Torah in adapted form,[431] like the Ten Commandments, not mentioned indeed in the Koran but recognizable in many comparable prescriptions anyway.[432] However, many of his improvements have been undone again by later generations of Moslems.[433]

In the previous pages I compared the image of man in the Koran with the image of man in the Torah. To sum up the following can be concluded:

> The element of partnership between God and man, so characteristic of the Torah, is absent in the Koran. The relation between Allah and man in the Koran is a relation of a Lord and his servant. The servant must submit completely to his Lord. Therefore in the Koran human life is especially seen in terms of obedience and disobedience and not in terms of a continuing development of learning, studying and trying out.

> In the Islam the completion of the creation doesn't play an essential part whatsoever, not to mention an active, independent contribution of man to it. After all, man's final destination is – according to the Koran – the paradise, that is in heaven.

> The thought that man through a process of learning contributes to a growing insight into what is good and what is evil, and that he should work at his own perfection, doesn't play a part in the Koran. The Koran reveals what is good and what is evil, what man must believe and what prescriptions he must keep to live well. Study and knowledge is the field of Islamic scholars, not of laymen. Laymen should limit themselves with obeying the five pillars of the Islam.

➢ Prayer is in the Islam ritualistically reciting and listening to Allah's words from the Koran, learning them by heart and submitting to them. Prayer hasn't the character of reflecting actively on oneself to support the human assignment to help to improve life and the world, as is the case in Judaism. The Islamic prayer consists of the words of the Koran and doesn't know a prayer book that is receptive to changes and that contains texts which are composed by men. Prayer is especially a public demonstration of faith in Allah, of asking for divine forgiveness of sins and of reciting the acknowledgement that Allah is merciful and gracious.

➢ Also justice and mercy fulfil another part in the Koran than in the Torah. Benevolence and brotherhood are not so much an aspect of universal humanity, but are especially concerned with the own Islamic society. They are principally values the Moslems should observe among themselves[a, 434]

➢ Also peace or well-being, which should be worked at with the ultimate aim the perfection of the world, don't play any part in the Koran. A messianic realm which has room for all people which respect the Torah, whether or not they accept it, is a concept not sufficient for the Koran. Only then one can speak of a global realm of peace when Islamic authority has been established in all societies of the earth.

The main criticism one could pass from Judaism and from modern Christianity on the Islam, is that the image of man in the Koran is an image of submission to a last and definitive revelation to which all people should surrender.[b] Consequently the creative responsibility for the improvement and perfection of the creation is going to be beyond the reach of human possibilities. But an open dialogue won't be possible either, because the final result of such a dialogue should be the

---

a   In the Koran the word "stranger" as someone who should be protected, is missing (see endnote). In the Torah however, the stranger is regularly taken under its protection.

b   This criticism concerns m.m. orthodox Christianity as well.

acceptance of the Islam by all people taking part in the dialogue. It remains to be seen whether more modern forms of Islam will be possible with a less rigid image of man than the traditional form, a more modern form that accepts an equal place for other religions, even when Moslems form the majority of a society.

Modern non-religious images of man

On the 1st of Januari 2004 the Law on Labour and Social Security came into effect in the Netherlands. This law intends to get unemployed people to work again, people who run the risk to end up in the social security system. In the years before 2004 civil servants of the Social Welfare services had to supply these people with State-financed social security. Too often this caused an uncritical, compliant attitude towards clients who came to appeal to social security. The new law provides the local authorities with a fixed budget for the benefits ánd for getting the unemployed to work again. If and when the local authorities have some money left, they are allowed to keep it to spend it on other welcome things.

After two years this law appeared to be a success, because it challenged the local authorities to intensify their efforts to get the unemployed to work again. The Municipal Social Welfare services have been converted into Municipal Services for Work and Income, set up as organizations directed at activation, with man at its centre. This law assumed "another image of man", at least so the media said,[435] and made a stronger appeal to the unemployed's responsibility to earn their income by working instead of living off society.

It rarely happens that the idea "image of man" plays an explicit, explanatory part in the media's coverage of social and political questions. Even less often is a certain position defended in the public and politic debate with an explicit appeal to the discussant's image of man. After all, this will make him vulnerable to his adversaries! And yet the image of man in which the solution to a social or political problem is looked for, may be the major success factor for the effects of that solution. If we want to better understand the part those images of man play in the public debate, it will also be necessary to investigate the dominant non-religious images of man of our society and culture next to the major religious images of man. That's the reason why I want to pay attention to this phenomenon in this section, so that some comparison with the image of man in the Torah will be made possible. Undoubtedly the briefness of the discourse will be accompanied by a lack of nuance and completeness. But who wants to discover something will be obliged to restrict himself, because the simple fact is that the overall reality is too big and too complex to encompass it completely.

Our western culture is not based on one, homogeneous image of man. Since the Renaissance various other images of man have been developed in Western Europe and America as alternatives for the orthodox-Christian image of man. They are very often conflicting, they compete with one another and some of them have greatly influenced the world. In the first place there is the rationalistic image of man that since the work of the French philosopher René Descartes (1596-1650) has laid the foundation of the development of Western philosophy and science.

The orthodox Roman Catholic doctrine made and still makes the assumption of the insufficiency of man's own conscience. Consequently, man should concentrate on and submit to the tradition of the Church. When Martin Luther (1483-1546), one of the founders of the Reformation showed the inconsistency of the Catholic religious tradition, a religious power vacuum was the result. However, Luther remained of the opinion that the individual man was not able to distinguish between true and not true, and not able to reach real knowledge. In his opinion this inability was removed by the revelation of the Scripture. So Luther and the Reformation didn't assume the intrinsic power of the human mind.[436]

Instead of submission to the Christian faith, Descartes focussed in his philosophy on the powers of the human mind, the human reason, central in his philosophy. His method of systematic doubt undermined all traditional certainties and existing institutes. This approach of Descartes' has been extremely renewing. Its consequence was an enormous revolution in the political and religious life, simultaneously with the development of sciences.[437]

In times before him, philosophical thinking concentrated on knowing the reality beyond man. Descartes' thinking, however, is directed at man's inner consciousness in which the world is being represented.[438] So, no longer the world but man occupies the centre stage of philosophy. According to Descartes man is especially a thinking being and the world is nothing but "extensiveness" to be measured by man,[439] the result being that human consciousness and the material world will be separated. In Descartes' view, real knowledge can only exist of inherent knowledge and knowledge deducible from this. The sensory world doesn't provide us with knowledge. Only when there is in our consciousness something like "idées claires et distinctes" (clear and distinct ideas) the gap between consciousness and the material world will be bridged.[440]

Descartes distinguished between the *res cogitans*, the reality of human thought, and the *res extensa*, the material reality. There is a principal distance between them, they don't constitute a unity.[441] Consequently the subject (man) *faces* an object (the world). That object can only be known as far as it can be measured and as far as it complies with the laws of mathematics and mechanics, since these are the laws of the thinking subject ("idées claires et distinctes"). This is the true knowledge of the measuring mind.[442]

The consequences of Descartes' philosophy for the rationalistic image of man are twofold. In the first place an almost absolute separation between body and mind comes into being. Instead of forming an entity as in the image of man in the Torah – observing, thinking, knowing, feeling, learning, acting – man is broken up into a thinking mind with mathematical powers and a body that can be examined as a mechanical instrument. In the next centuries attempts are made to approach the "mind" also with scientific methods. In the end the behaviourism of the psychologist J.B Watson (1878-1958) wants to explain even the psyche entirely from mechanical stimulus-response patterns. Only in the second half of the 20th century new insights arise in the cognitive psychology influenced by computer science, on how the human mind works. Internally represented programs and purposive strategies become, in that case, possible again as models of explanation and the interests in intentional and teleological explanations of behaviour grow again.[443] But also nowadays the Descartian distinction between body and mind is still a source of problems for the basis of the psychology and other social sciences.[444] In medical science and in the health services one still starts working – either consciously or unconsciously – from this body-and-mind paradigm, which in the first place causes the care to begin with the body, the mind being considered secondary.

In the second place a de-moralization of the scientific image of man takes place from Descartes. After all, ethics, the knowledge how to act, don't belong to the domain of the "idées claires et distinctes", which we can make ourselves familiar with scientific methods. Descartes puts ethics, as possible source of errors and imperfections, in brackets. If there is no longer a divine or natural design for ethics, man will be the inventor of his own ethics, instead of being the discoverer of the divine or natural ethics. For even Descartes takes the view that man simply can't live without ethics. A number of virtues is all that is left, virtues like: obeying the laws and customs of the country one lives in; acting resolutely even when the foundation for it is not sure; self-control and devoting one's life to philosophy.[445]

Descartes doesn't offer a clear moral philosophy. This was left to his followers, among them Immanuel Kant (1724-1804). In his *Kritik der praktischen Vernunft* (Critique of Pure Reason) he studies the human ability to act and he distinguishes between the behaviour of man following his impulse and being a slave of his passions, and the behaviour of man being guided by reason and acting according to a rule, or as Kant states: (man) "acting according to a maxim of the will".[446, a] One of his propositions is: act in such a way that you could wish the maxim of your acting to become a general law. Kant, for instance, takes the view that a criminal should be punished even after an

---

a   A maxim is a concise description, a basic rule or an aphorism.

unhappy youth, because if punishment is withheld, he isn't taken seriously as a person. But even Kant hasn't been able to save the scientific image of man from de-moralization, which, in the 19th century took on new, more radical forms in, for instance, the theory of evolution of Charles Darwin (1809-1882), the psychoanalysis of Sigmund Freud (1856-1939) and the historical materialism of Karl Marx (1818-1883), three theories which have extraordinarily influenced the world ever since.

Darwin's theory of evolution contributed in the 19th century that man was seen more and more as an animal improved by natural selection. Even though Darwin himself was vague about religious and moral questions, yet his theories were accepted with open arms by all sorts of groups as support for their social and political ideas. Darwin's idea that nature consists of a collection of individuals, with each individual fighting, egoistically, for his own survival, was parallelled by 19th century liberalism, that didn't want to allow the Government to make laws, which would impede a citizen's freedom. Darwinism seemed to supply a scientific basis for free competition. For Marxists it was attractive that Darwinism acknowledged material surroundings as the decisive factor in human development. The imperialists saw the law of the jungle confirmed by this theory and the racial theorists derived from it the right of dominance of superior races.[447] These are the reasons why Darwinism has had an enormous influence on social, political and phylosophical field,[448] and it still has.[a] Adherents of the theory of evolution are, by and large, blind to the fact that in the history of the human species not only *natural selection* plays a part, but that also morality and ethical behaviour could be well of overriding importance for the way in which human society develops.

Freud too, contributed with the development of psychoanalysis in his way to the de-moralization of the western culture. The soul is in his

---

a The debat that flared up not so long ago in the Dutch House of Commons on the Theory of Evolution versus Intelligent Design makes it likely that Darwinism is still an important support for the political and philosophical ideas of some politicians.

view a battlefield where the powers of the subconsciousness are regulated via sublimation and repression. Human feelings of lust and aggression, which originally would have resulted in socially unacceptable behaviour, should be suppressed (suppression) or canalized in such a way that they are expressed in a socially acceptable way (sublimation). Both mechanisms form the basis of the process of civilization, but are also forms of repression which can cause neuroses. It's the psychoanalist's task to help patients to come to terms with such traumas. The psychoanalysis however, is not interested in ethics: patients are neither right or wrong. They are only the victims of a conflict between the inclinations of their subconsciousness and the demands of society as represented in their consciousness. They are not responsible at all for the development of this inner conflict. Patients who suffer from lack of sense and meaning in their lives won't be helped essentially by psychoanalysis.[449]

Perhaps not one of all these theories, developed in the 19th century, has more strongly influenced the world than Marxism. In his work Marx did not only want to describe society and its origin, but he also wanted to show the way how this could and should develop into a more decent society.[450] His theory has a historicistic character: in his opinion history is a process, the course of which is inescapable and can be predicted accordingly. In a sense, Marx's image of man was an optimistic one. He thought that in the right material circumstances and with the right education of the proletariat the "Utopia" or the "ideal state" should come into being accordingly. The human mind, he thought, was malleable and in the right social relations a "new man" should arise, free from egoistic, bad characteristics. Then exploitation, oppression and war would belong to the past. The state, a tool of oppression according to Marx, could disappear gradually.[451]

The compelling character of the historical development sketched by Marx, results in the fact that man as a responsibly acting individual matters very little. In the more steeled versions of Marx' doctrine this leads to the elimination of each and every normative problem. No real problems of choice occur, because the outcome of social development is fixed. The question whether a social intervention is justified, is no longer relevant, because such an intervention in society only accelerates or slackens the course of history. After all, the birth of a new society is unavoidable.[452]

This perspective allowed Bertold Brecht the famous maxim: "Zuerst das Fressen, dann die Moral", i.e. "The grub first, morals next". This maxim pithily reflects the Marxist image of man: man's economical circumstances determine his moral attitude; fight poverty first, social behaviour will follow automatically. But in this way man is devaluated to a biological being whose chief concern is to survive without concerning himself about his morals, about how he associates with his fellow men. Today the influence of this idea can be recognized in some leftist circles which manage to have a great deal of understanding for certain movements which under the cover of resistance against oppression and poverty often wage a relentless war with amoral means like taking hostages, car bombs and suicide attacks.

In the Marxist view man is at the collective level of society also devaluated to a member of the "human stock", kept by the state and the party. The state takes care of the "grub", the "morals" that should follow, are the regime's morals. And so it has been in communist countries for decades and it still is in countries like China, North Korea and Cuba. Nowhere Marxism has brought the liberation Marx expected, on the contrary, it has lead to the worst forms of oppression, just because the Marxist image of man is no good!

The moral emptiness, called into being by rationalism, Darwinism, psychoanalysis and Marxism was the breeding ground for a strong countermovement in the European culture. Already in the 18th century some people discovered that the image of man of rationalism was, after all, an anaemic thing. So in the 18th and 19th century German Romanticism came into being in reaction to the rationalistic, often French, urban culture with its imperialistic foreign policy.[453] The major representative of this German Romanticism, Johann Gottfried von Herder (1744-1803), believed that nations are organic communities which had developed like trees, rooted in their native soil. Their languages and culture each had a soul, unique for each community. Old wisdom and primordially human virtues were embedded in these communities, in their language and in the *Volksgeist* which gave them life. However, in their opinion the European world had become bleak, frozen by the French philosophy of universal reason. By contrast Von Herder considered the nations in the tropical continents as "natural children", who still worshipped gods and powerful, wise men. Compared with Europe primitive societies were better off, purer and more authentic, he thought. The European idea of freedom led in his view only to inhumanity and fruitless materialism.[454]

This German Romanticism and its romantic nationalism are, according to the political philosopher and historian Isaiah Berlin (1901-1997), the product of an injured national humiliation due to the French domination of Europe, political, cultural and military. The German romanticists created an opposition between their own "profound, spiritual life", the "simplicity and nobility of their national character", the "poetry of their national soul", and the emptiness, cruelty and artificiality of French rationalism. This was accompanied by a "return" to real or imaginary triumphs from the German past.[455] Romanticism was a kind of anti-Enlightment movement. When thinkers of the Enlightment are optimistic and consider history a linear progress to a more rational world, romanticists use old religious notions like the original guiltlessness and grandeur of man, his decline in the present juncture and his liberation in a glorious future. Romanticists feel as if they find themselves at the absolute low of the decline. This decline is a condition of fragmentation and estrangement from one's own inner nature, from one's fellow man, from one's outer nature and from God. Romanticism is always nostalgic: the past is always more beautiful than the present and the future should become like this again: restoration of unity and harmony. In this view "organic" is a good word, "mechanical" a bad one.[456]

In the second half of the 19th century after Germany had defeated the French in 1871, the German romantic idealism gets an explicit militaristic character. From then on the *Deutsche Kultur*, "culture in the German way", takes the shape of heroism and bellicose, disciplinary self-sacrifice.[457] The result of which we saw halfway through the 20th century: the roots of the Nazism of Hitler-Germany, the Second World War and ultimately the holocaust were found for the greater part in the image of man of the German Romanticism. Romanticism as a countermovement against the cold rationalism has ultimately produced the monstrous, national-socialistic image of man as a disciplined soldier-labourer, a leaflet on the huge tree of the people's collective, the party, the *Volksgeist*, the state, the race, the Leader.

Romantic poets have always craved for the pastoral Arcadia and have always detested the modern, commercial, urban societies of the West.[458] Incidentally, the influence of German Romanticism as countermovement to the rationalistic and liberal culture of Western Europe and America has not been restricted to the Germany of about 1800 alone. The 19th century Russian philosophers were highly influenced by German Romanticism, too. They developed a model for nationally and ethnically inspired attacks on Western rationalism which would also be used, later, by generations of intellectuals in India, China and the Islamic world.[459] Even Marxism with its *Verelendung* (immiseration) of the proletariat and its utopia of the classless society can be taken as a rationalistic form of Romanticism. In the 20th century Romanticism greatly influenced all anti-Western movements, in and outside Europe, whether they had Marxist or nationalistic characters. Even today many people let themselves be inspired in their anti-Western propaganda by the anti-Semitic and Nazi excrescences of the German Romanticism with its heroism and bellicose, disciplinary self-sacrifice.[460, a]

The rationalistic and the romantic images of man I have drawn above, make themselves strongly felt, even today, not only in our Western society but in the whole world. However, a full discussion of it lies beyond the scope of this book. That's why at the end of this sec-

---

a   Prof.Dr. P.W. van der Horst rightly pointed out in his farewell speech at Utrecht University (spring 2006) that European intellectuals and the Western media are, in general, heedless of the anti-Semitism in the Arabic world.

tion I'm restricting myself to one example that received some attention in the media some years ago.

The English psychiatrist and social critic Theodore Dalrymple (pen name of Anthony M. Daniels, born 1949), is one of the few scientists who dare involve the moral behaviour of people in their analysis of social problems nowadays.[461] He states for instance that the many suicides, drug addictions and manifestations of crimes in the dregs of our society stem from the spiritual poverty the lower social strata languish in. Many of them aren't lacking in material prosperity, but their lives are empty and meaningless. This is caused partly by the welfare state which keeps many of these people alive as "pet animals" by providing them with benefits which allow them to briefly enjoy drink, drugs, violent and criminal kicks and alternating sexual relations. But also the intellectual upper class of the population is to be blamed, because it no longer points the way to society, because they submerse in cultural relativism. There is no standard of civilization left, kept up by people from the upper class, which people from the subclass can try to reach to improve their life. Besides, the result of the lack of such a standard is that someone can no longer fail in his duty to himself or to his fellow men anymore. According to Dalrymple this causes a devaluation of achievements and examinations in education. Why should one try and excel? After all, why should someone who performs poorly *not* get a diploma?

In the social sciences which have dominated our social (way of) thought for half a century, free will is consequently left behind according to Dalrymple, because it can't be measured so it can't explain human behaviour. All man's behaviour ought to be explained by factors like income, gender, genetical material, social position etc. Here we see the influence of the rationalistic and of the Marxist image of man coalesce. The result being that one is inclined to consider people who misbehave to be victims instead of offenders.

Dalrymple reports how the subclass has become aware of these ideas, and has begun to use them as self-justification for one's own and one another's misbehaviour. He especially reproaches a lot of Western intellectuals and artists and considers them to be responsible for this phenomenon. Influenced as they are by the romantic sides of Marxist thought, many among them believe that people are good by nature, but that they are deformed by the social and economic circumstances they live in, and consequently won't be responsible themselves. It is denied – or simply overlooked – that a social meaningful and successful life is the result of generations of education, history of civilization and passing on culture. According to Dalrymple man is not good by nature and freedom doesn't automatically bring about the good life. We should be careful about our civilization in order to prevent nihilism's emptiness.

So it wouldn't be wrong to research the social and intellectual success of groups, related to the image of man they live with.

The image of man in the Torah as a "third" path

In the first two sections of this chapter I have discussed the images of man in orthodox Christianity and in the Koran. In the previous section I've drawn an image of the rationalistic and romantic image of man in the modern, secular, Western culture. Now these two groups of images of man are extraordinarily in contrast with one another. The images of man of orthodox Christianity and Islam are characterized by man being subordinate to a divine diktat. Conversely the secular images of man of rationalism and Romanticism confine man to his individual and collective consciousness respectively. Our modern society is the product of the struggle the adherents of all those images of man experienced in the past centuries, and in which they still detain each other. Few theologians and philosophers have showed interest for the fact that in our Western world another, a third image of man has been at work as leaven: the image of man in the Torah and in Judaism.

Elsewhere I have explained the topicality of the image of man in the Torah and how well it fits into today's reality.[462] It doesn't start from a hierarchically, but from a democratically organized society. It highlights people's individual responsibility and calls on to public spirit and social justice at the same time. It hardly has a metaphysical attitude, but it does have a highly ethical one with regard to human existence. It shows an empirically accepting attitude in relation to the reality of life (taken as the reality of the God given Creation) and at the same time a readiness to take action to improve the Creation as a partner in the creation process. It is based on the equality of all people and strives to solve conflicts using as less violence as possible. Finally, in the image of man in the Torah, man is a learning being that should go on developing itself permanently. On the basis of which I would even say that the essential features of modern Western society have already existed in Judaism for ages and that we will be able to learn a lot of the Jewish experiences with the image of man in the Torah.

For those who want to avoid the problematic choice between spiritual submission (orthodox Christianity and Islam) and ethical arbitrariness (rationalism and Romanticism), the Torah offers a third path in my view. The Torah is indeed the fruit of divine revelation, but a revelation people of free will can work with, as partners in the perfection of the human situation. The image of man in the Torah recognizes the awareness of sin and atonement, it doesn't need the sacrificial death of a mediator. It does indeed take faithfulness for granted, but not submission. The image of man in the Torah stimulates man's intellectual powers, but doesn't restrict them to reason. It imposes on him responsibility for society, but doesn't make the individual man subservient to the national community. On the strength of the image of man in the Torah, people will always be and remain responsible to act morally. Poverty isn't a licence for robbery either. Suppression doesn't morally entitle people to murder and terror. Whoever has a morally principled society in mind, will have to use morally responsible means. The image of man in the Torah has much to offer to both Jews and non-Jews today.

Notes

1   A concise overview of this extensive literature could be found in: Musaph-Andriesse, 1982.

2   Mekilta de-Rabbi Ishmael 19, 2 (Lauterbach, 1976).

3   Ginzberg, 1968-1969, Vol. III, p. 90.

4   See e.g.: Aschkenasy & Whitlau, 1981, p. 23.

5   Aschkenasy & Whitlau, 1981, p. 15-16.

6   See the story about the difference of opinion between Rabbi Eli'ezer and the other Rabbis in bT Baba Metsia 59b (I discussed it in: Van 't Riet, 2012, section 1.5).

7   See: De Bruin, 1983, p. 111.

8   M. Sanhedrin 4:5.

9   See e.g.: Abram, 1980, p. 130 f.

10 Abram. 1980, p. 131.

11 Evers, 1998, p. 47

12 Evers, 1998, p. 54

13 Evers, 1998, p. 66

14 Free quotation borrowed from Vreekamp, 1987, p. 29.

15 See e.g.: Van der Sluis e.a., 1978, p. 1 f.

16 bT Sotah 14a; bT Baba Metsia 86b. See also: Ginzberg, part I, 1968, p. 240.

17 Genesis Rabba 48, 1.

18 Rashi loc.,

19 See e.g. Ginzberg, vol. VII, 1968, p. 332.

20 Herzberg, 1977, p. 83 f.

21 Evers, 1998, p. 14.

22 De Vries, 1968, p. 13-14.

23 bT. Mêgillah 26b-27a; Scheepstra, 1983, p. 8.

24 Millgram, 1975, p. 15-16.

25 Buber & Rosenzweig, 1954.

26 Abram, 1980, p. 77-78.

27 Exodus Rabba 41:6 (Freedman & Simon, 1961).

28 Abram, 1980, p. 91-92.

29 E.g. in: bT. Gittin 60b.

30 Glatzer, 1966, p. 55; see also: Boertien, 1974, p. 14.

31 bT. Yêvamot 71a; bT. Baba Metsia 31b.

32 Abram, 1980, p. 94.

33 Abram, 1980, p. 81.

34 M. Avot 5:22.

35 Abram, 1980, p. 76.

36 Abram, 1980, p. 82.

37 Cf. Levinas, 1969, p. 60.

38 Barnard & Van 't Riet, 1986, p. 33 f.

39 See also: Abram, 1980, p. 77.

40 Abram, 1980, p. 101-102.

41 Beentjes, 1982, p.33-34. On different opinions see e.g. Scheepstra, 1983, p. 16, as opposed to Boertien, 1974, p. 12.

42 Abram, 1980, p. 69. Abram uses the term 'permanent education'. I, however, use 'learning all one's life'.

43 bT. Ta'anit 7a.

44 bT. Ta'anit 7a.

45 Abram, 1980, p. 118.

46 Abram, 1980, p. 157.

47 ARN 17 (Goldin, 1967).

48 Abram, 1980, p. 150; see for the following passages also: Idem, p. 246 f.

49 Hertz, 1976, p. 614.

50 M. Avot 1: 4.

51 bT. Sabbath 119b.

52 Abram, 1980, p. 250.

53 Hirsch, 1978, p. 418.

54 M. Avot 1:1.

55 Van Tijn, 1988, p. 44.

56 Lehmann, 1963, p. 14.

57 ARN 3 (Goldin, 1957, p. 44-45).

58 Lehmann, 1963, p. 14.

59 bT. Choelin 133a; see also: Goldin, 1957, p. 45.

60 bT. Bêrachot 63a; see also: Glatzer, 1966, p. 30.

61 Free translation of M. Avoth 1:11.

62 M. Avoth 1:3.

63 bT. Nêdariem 49b; see also: Prijs, 1980, p. 33, 37 nt. 5.

64 Lehmann, 1963, p. 13-15.

65 Travers Herford, 1969, p. 21.

66 Neusner, 1975, p. 70.

67 Brienen, 1990, p. 48-49.

68 bT Kiddushin 30b.

69 Abram, 1980, p. 136-138.

70 M. Avot 2:5.

71 Brienen, 1990, p. 60.

72 M. Bêrachot 1:1.

73 Brienen, 1990, p. 43.

74 Brienen, 1990, p. 46.

75 Abram, 1980, p. 117.

76 Rosen, 2001, p. 40.

77 Abram, 1980, p. 134-135.

78 bT. Sabbath 199b.

79 pT. Chagigah I, 7, 76c.

80 bT. Megillah 26b-27a; see also: Scheepstra, 1983, p. 8.

81 Scheepstra, 1983, p. 9-13.

82 Scheepstra, 1983, p. 13, 15, 21.

83 Abram, 1980, p. 151.

84 Abram, 1980, p. 154-155.

85 bT. Baba Batra 21a.

86 Scheepstra, 1983, p. 10-11.

87 Abram, 1980, p. 156.

88 bT. Ta'aniet 7a.

89 Abram, 1980, p. 157-158.

90 M. Avot 3:6.

91 M. Avot1:6; Abram , 1980, p. 158-159.

92 Abram, 1980, p. 165-168.

93 Evers, 1998, p. 20.

94 M. Avot 1:1.

95 bT. Kiddushin 40b.

96 Glazer, 1966, p. 48.

97 M. Pe'ah 1:1.

98 bT. Kiddushin 39b; ARN 40.

99   Abram, 1980, p. 125.

100 Abram, 1980, p. 96.

101 Abram, 1980, p. 113.

102 bT. Bêrachot 17a.

103 Abram , 1980, p. 130-132.

104 M. Avot 2:4.

105 bT. Nidda 16b.

106 ARN2 2; Goldin, 1957, p. 20.

107 Abram, 1980, p. 129.

108 Abram, 1980, p. 161.

109 Abram, 1980, p. 161 e.v.

110 Abram, 1980, p. 219.

111 Abram, 1980, p. 126-128.

112 Rashi to Genesis 11:5.

113 bT. Sota 14b.

114 Aschkenasy and Whitlau, 1981, p. 18.

115 bT. Mênachot 110a.

116 Abram, 1980, p. 112.

117 C.E. (1), below: Bidden.

118 De Lepper, 1950, p. 92-93, 101.

119 See e.g.: Wegman, 1983, p. 29-30.

120 See for the full quotation in Dutch: C.E. (1), below: Bidden.

121 See e.g.: Van der Meer, 1970, passim.

122 Kushner, 1993, p. 127, 134.

123 Hausdorff, 1977, p. IV.

124 Soetendorp, 1953, p. 121; Peli, 1988, p. 9.

125 Peli, 1988, p. 8.

126 Hausdorff, 1977, p. V-VI.

127 Millgram, 1975, p. 9-10.

128 Van Uden, 1978, p. 3-4.

129 Maimonides, Misjné Tora, Hilchot Tefila 1, 1.

130 Van Uden, 1978, p. 4 en 9.

131 Van Uden, 1978, p. 35.

132 Peli, 1988, p. 5.

133 Millgram, 1975, p. 3.

134 Hausdorff, 1977, p. XX.
135 Millgram, 1975, p. 5-8; Soetendorp, 1953, p. 125.
136 The English translation is taken from the Encyclopedia of Jewish Concepts. For the full text in Dutch, see: Van der Sluis e.o., 1978, p. 14-19.
137 Hausdorff, 1977, p. XVIII-XIX.
138 Hausdorff, 1977, p. XVI.
139 Peli, 1988, p. 11.
140 Van Uden, 1978, p. 15.
141 bT. Berachot 43b. See also: Prijs, 1980, p. 24-25.
142 bT. Berachot 54a.
143 Millgram, 1975, p. 13-15.
144 Kushner, 1993, p. 134.
145 Van Uden, 1978, p. 22.
146 Peli, 1988, p. 12.
147 Van Uden, 1978, p. 23-24.
148 Hausdorff, 1977, p. XVII.
149 Peli, 1988, p. 12.
150 Peli, 1988, p. 13.
151 Midrash Tehillim to Psalm 31:21 (Braude, 1959, p. 398).
152 Millgram, 1975, p. 33.
153 M. Sota 7:1.
154 Millgram, 1975, p. 34.
155 Kushner, 1993, p. 128-130.
156 Millgram, 1975, p. 17.
157 Van Uden, 1978, p. 5.
158 Kushner, 1993, p. 130.
159 M. Bêrachot 4:3
160 Millgram, 1975, p. 26-27.
161 Kushner, 1993, p. 130; Millgram, 1975, p. 28.
162 Peli, 1988, p. 6.
163 Peli, 1988, p. 19.
164 Millgram, 1975, p. 32.
165 bT. Mêgilla 25a.
166 Peli, 1988, p. 23.
167 Hausdorff, 1977, p. IX.

168 Hausdorff, 1977, p. XIII.
169 bT. Jêwamot 64a.
170 Heschel, 1954, p. 12; Millgram, 1975, p. 25; Peli, 1988, p. 10-11; Soetendorp, 1953, p. 123.
171 Soetendorp, 1953, p. 124.
172 Hausdorff, 1977, p. XII.
173 Hausdorff, 1977, p. VI-VII.
174 Van Uden, 1978, p. 31-32.
175 Millgram, 1975, p. 27.
176 Van Uden, 1978, p. 8.
177 M. Bêrachot 5:1; Millgram, 1975, p. 28
178 M. Bêrachot 7b-8a.
179 Millgram, 1975, p. 30.
180 bT. Bêrachot 29b-30a.
181 Millgram, 1975, p. 31.
182 Van Uden, 1978, p. 33-34.
183 Kushner, 1993, p. 132.
184 Van Uden, 1978, p. 35.
185 bT. Bêrachot 54a.
186 Millgram, 1975, p. 12.
187 Millgram, 1975, p. 13.
188 Van Uden, 1978, p. 21.
189 Kushner, 1993, p. 134-135
190 Hausdorff, 1977, p. X.
191 Hausdorff, 1977, p. XI.
192 Evers, 1998, p. 22.
193 Soetendorp, 1953, p. 121.
194 Soetendorp, 1953, p. 121.
195 Kadushin, 1964, p. 126, quoted in: Deen, 1990, p. 45.
196 Van Uden, 1978, p. 26.
197 Soetendorp, 1953, p. 126.
198 Millgram, 1975, p. 6.
199 Millgram, 1975, p. 15-16.
200 Kushner, 1993, p. 135-136.
201 Deen, 1990, p. 45-46.

202 Peli, 1988, p. 7.
203 Hausdorff, 1977, p. XIX-XX.
204 Kushner, 1993, p. 133.
205 Peli, 1988, p. 14.
206 Hausdorff, 1977, p. XIV-XVI.
207 Soetendorp, 1953, p. 124-125.
208 Soetendorp, 1953, p. 123; zie ook: jT. Bêrachot 9, 1.
209 Peli, 1988, p. 10.
210 Millgram, 1975, p. 21-23.
211 R.u.T., at: Armut.
212 See e.g.: N.K., 1966, p. 509, "De eerste en fundamentele liefde tot de medemens in nood is dat men diens recht zoekt." ("The first and fundamental love for the neighbour in need is that on should look for his right."
213 For the first paragraphes of this section I refer to e.g.: Mayer, 1980, p. 460-463.
214 M. Avot 1:2.
215 Maarsen, 1932, p. 20; Polak & Mulder, 1862, p. 106.
216 Hirsch, 1978, p. 419.
217 ARN 4.
218 Hertz, 1976, p. 615.
219 Buber & Rosenzweig, 1954: "Halte lieb deinen Genossen, dir gleich".
220 jT. Nedarim 9, 3.
221 See for the above: Prijs, 1980, p. 15.
222 E.g. bT Shabbath 31a; see also: Evers, 1998, p. 53.
223 T.D.O.T., at: áhàv.
224 bT. Baba Metsia 59b.
225 bT. Chagigah 59a.
226 Prijs, 1980, p. 16.
227 bT. Bêrachot 17a.
228 Resh-Ayin-He; Gesenius, 1962, q.v.
229 The following is a somewhat free translation of bT Bêrachot 10a.
230 bT. Soekah 49b. See also: Goldin, 1957, p. 47-48.
231 Maarsen, 1932, p. 21.
232 Much of this paragraph has been borrowed from: Evers, 1998, p. 50-58.
233 Much of this paragraph has been borrowed from: Evers, 1998, p. 26-34.

234 bT. Ta'anit 23a-b freely rendered.

235 Evers, 1998, p. 29-30.

236 bT. Sukkah 49b; bT. Bava Batra 9a.

237 Tos. Peah 4:19.

238 bT. Shabbath 118a.

239 Much of this section has been derived from: E.J., at: Charity; Poor, Provision for the.

240 Tos. Peah 2:13.

241 Leviticus Rabbah 34:8.

242 bT. Kêtubot 67b.

243 bT. Gittin 7a.

244 Shulchan Aruch, Yorei Deah 251:3.

245 bT. Peah 5:4.

246 bT. Peah 8:8.

247 bT. Baba Kamma 7a-b.

248 bT. Kêtubot 50a.

249 bT. Kêtubot 67a.

250 bT. Chagigah 5a.

251 bT. Baba Batra 10a.

252 M. Shêkalim 5:6.

253 bT. Ta'anit 21b. See also: E.J., at: Abba Umana.

254 bT. Kêtubot 67b.

255 Maimonides, Mishneh Torah, Seeds 10:7-12.

256 Idem, 9:1-3.

257 bT. Baba Batra 8a, 9a.

258 bT. Pêsachim 112a, 113a.

259 Much in this section has been taken taken from: De Vries, 1968, p. 250 ff.

260 bT. Joma 85a-b.

261 Hausdorff. 1977, p. XI.

262 De Vries, 1968, p. 255.

263 See for the above paragraph: De Vries, 1968, p. 255-256.

264 bT. Bêrachot 10a.

265 The contents of this section has been derived from: De Vries, 1968, p. 258 ff.

266 The theme of this section has been derived from: De Vries, 1968, p. 263 ff.

267 See: De Vries, 1968, p. 290-295.

268 E.J., lemma: Peace; Van den Born, 1966-1969, lemma: peace (I).

269 Pedersen, 1926, p. 311-314.

270 Cf. 2 Samuel 17:3; Micha 5:4; Job 5:24.

271 This translation is – with some variations – based on: Dasberg, 1977, p. 138.

272 Schelling, 2002.

273 Aschkenasy et al., 2001-2002, p. 166.

274 See also: Van den Born, 1966-1969, lemma: Peace (I).

275 Van den Born, 1966-1969, lemma: Peace (I).

276 Van 't Riet, 1996, p. 284-287.

277 See: E.J., Lemma: Sacrifice, Peace Offerings.

278 G.F. Moore quoted in: Van der Sluis et al., 1978, p. 368.

279 E.J., lemma: Peace, In the Talmud.

280 M. Avoth 1:18.

281 bT. Bêrachoth 64a.

282 Leviticus Rabbah 9:9.

283 bT. Shabbat 10b.

284 M. Uktzin 3:12.

285 Sifre Numbers 6:26 section 42 (12b); see also: Van der Sluis et al., 1978, p. 366; Strack-Billerbeck, 1969, vol. I, p. 215 ff.

286 Sifre Numbers 6:26 section 42 (12b); see also: Strack-Billerbeck, 1969, vol. I, p. 215 e.v.

287 Leviticus Rabbah 9:9.

288 Pesikta de-Rav Kahana 12.

289 Urbach, 1979, p. 179-180.

290 M. Sanhedrin 4:5; see also: Urbach, 1979, p. 217.

291 Leviticus Rabbah 9:9; see also: Van der Sluis et al., 1978, p. 362.

292 Leviticus Rabbah 9 (110d); see also: Strack-Billerbeck, 1969, vol. I, p. 217-218.

293 bT. Yevamoth 65b.

294 Van Loopik, 1989, p. 104.

295 Genesis Rabbah 48; Leviticus Rabbah 9; Numbers Rabbah 11; bT. Yevamoth 65b.

296 Aschkenasy et al., 2001-2002, p. 177.

297 ARN 12.

298 Genesis Rabbah 54:3; see also: Aschkenasy et al., 2001-2002, p. 168-169.

299 See for the above: Urbach, 1979, p. 615.

300 M. Avot 1:12; cf. also bT. Yoma 71b.

301 ARN 12.

302 Urbach, 1979, p. 615. More about these dilemma's in: Aschkenasy et al., 2001-2002, p. 161-180.

303 Aschkenasy et al., 2001-2002, p. 172.

304 M. Sabbath 6:4.

305 Sifre Numbers 6:26 section 42 (12b). See also: Strack-Billerbeck, 1969, vol. I, 215 e.v.

306 M. Avoth 1:12.

307 M. Avoth 1:14; see also: Urbach, 1979, p. 589.

308 Lapide, 1983, p. 19-20.

309 Sifre Numbers 6:26 section 42 (12b) refering to Isaiah 57:2 and 48:22; see also: Strack-Billerbeck, 1969, vol. I, p. 215 e.v.

310 bT. Yevamoth 96b (translation based on: Van de Sluis et al. 1978, p. 361).

311 bT. Kiddushin 30b; see also: Abram, 1980, p. 136-137.

312 M. Avoth 5:17.

313 bT. Yevamoth 14b (Van der Sluis et al., 1978, p. 361).

314 Pesikta Rabbati 3.

315 See for the below mentioned: Strack-Billerbeck, 1969, vol. I, 380 ff.

316 For more information see e.g.: Strack-Billerbeck, 1969, vol. I, p. 384-385; Van Boxel, 1994, p. 102-103.

317 bT. Berachoth 17a.

318 M. Avoth 4:15.

319 Van Boxel, 1994, p. 103.

320 Bunim, 2000, vol. II, p. 589.

321 bT. Gittin 70b; M. Shevi'it 4:3.

322 Commentary to M. Gittin 5:9.

323 jT. Berachah 8, 12c, 46.

324 bT. Gittin 62a Baraitah.

325 Numbers Rabbah 8.

326 ARN 12 (translation based on: Van der Sluis et al., 1978, p. 357-358).

327 Van der Sluis et al., 1978, p. 359.

328 bT. Berachoth 12a.

329 Van der Sluis et al., 1978, p. 354. The translation of Numbers 6:24-26 is with some variations based on: Dasberg, 1977, p. 138.

330 Van der Sluis et al., 1978, p. 124.

331 Leviticus Rabbah 9, 9 (see also: Van der Sluis et al., 1978, p. 123).

332 Transaltion based on: Van der Sluis et al., 1978, p. 351.

333 Van der Sluis et al., 1978, p. 123.

334 E. Landshuth in siddoer Hegyon Lev (see: Van der Sluis et al., 1978, p. 355-356).

335 Van der Sluis et al., 1978, p. 357.

336 Van der Sluis et al., 1978, p. 352.

337 Translation based on: Petuchowski, 1987, p. 49.

338 See e.g.: Van 't Riet, 2001, p. 147 ff.

339 See e.g. the beautiful consideration in: Rosen, 2001, p. 95-97.

340 Den Heyer, 1983, p. 62-63.

341 Midrasj ha-Gadol on Numbers 6:26; cf. also: Genesis Rabbah 66:2 (Van der Sluis et al., 1978, p. 366-367).

342 Van der Sluis et al., 1978, p. 366-367.

343 Van der Sluis et al, 1978, p. 368-369.

344 Buber, 1967, p. 164.

345 Elsewhere I wrote extensively about the image of man in Christianity. The text here is a somewhat altered passage from: Van 't Riet, 2001, p. 107 ff.

346 Barnard & Van 't Riet, 1986, p. 142 ff.

347 Berkhof, undated, p. 188 ff.

348 O.v.D., Heidelberg Catechism 3.8.

349 Berkhof, undated, p. 198 ff.

350 Berkhof, undated, p. 188 ff., devotes e.g. 10 pages to positive and 25 pages to the negative sides of being human.

351 Berkhof, undated, p. 200 and 219.

352 Köhler, 1967, p. 63 ff.

353 N.K., 1966, p. 312.

354 Weber, 1987, p. 658.

355 N.K., 1966, p. 311, 313, 530.

356 N.K., 1966, p. 313.

357 Weber, 1987, p. 654.

358 Berkhof, 1976, p. 82; E.E.K., 1977, p. 275.

359 Berkhof, undated, p. 203.

360 See for these two expressions: N.K., 1966, p. 305-306.

361 See for the last three expressions: Berkhof, 1976, p. 63, 81 en 85.

362 O.v.D., Heidelber Catechism 3, 8. See also: E.E.K., 1977, that speaks of: "voll böser Lust und Neigung" (p. 268).
363 Berkhof, undated, p. 204.
364 E.E.K., 1977, p. 257.
365 See e.g. O.v.D., The Heidelberg Catechism, Sundays 3 and 4; N.K., 1966, p. 304 ff., 528 ff.
366 Berkhof, 1976, p. 85.
367 Berkhof, 1976, p. 84 ff.
368 E.B. Mac., after: Christianity, p. 467 ff.; Berkhof, 1976, p. 83.
369 Weber, 1987, p. 677.
370 Berkhof, 1976, p. 85.
371 See e.g.: O.v.D., The Heidelberg Catechism 3, 8. Also: Berkhof, undated, p. 21 the 5th item.
372 See: Klein, 8 December 2000.
373 See e.g. in: Kuitert, 1971, p. 183, we read: "Because in 'the things concerning Jesus' (Luke 24:19) it's about the salvation of the guilty mankind, i.e. about the salvation that exposes mankind at the same time as guilty of the chaos in the world ... etc.". Later Kuitert developed his ideas subsequently indeed, but at the moment he wrote this he was reputed to be very modern in the Reformed Churches of The Netherlands.
374 Attema, 1962, p. 10; Beck, 2002, p. 69.
375 Beck, 2002, p. 65.
376 Beck, 2002, p. 65.
377 Abdus Sattar, 2003, p. 92.
378 Abdus Sattar, 2003, p. 93; Ayoub, 2005, p. 10-11.
379 Attema, 1962. p. 10-12.
380 See also: Beck, 2002, p. 72.
381 Wessels, 2006, p. 122-123.
382 Abdus Sattar, 2003, p. 15, who talks euphemistically about "somewhat recalcitrant".
383 Wessels, 2006, p. 120-121, 126.
384 Abdus Sattar, 2003, p. 18.
385 Wessels, 2006, p. 139.
386 Laffin, 1976, p. 87.
387 Buber & Rosenzweig, 1954, Volume I, p. 14.
388 This wording is a combination of the images from: Sura 7:19-25 and from: Abdus Sattar, 2003, p. 14.

389 Wessels, 2006, p. 126-128.
390 Ayoub, 2005, p. 31.
391 Wessels, 2006, p. 81-82.
392 Wessels, 2006, p. 86.
393 Wessels, 2006, p. 90-91.
394 Beck, 2002, p. 70.
395 Wessels, 2006, p. 133.
396 Attema, 1962, p. 77-79, 83.
397 Abdus Sattar, 2003, p. 27.
398 Abdus Sattar, 2003, p. 87.
399 Beck, 2002, p. 70-71.
400 Wessels, 2006, p. 110.
401 Ayoub, 2005, p. 8.
402 Wessels, 2006, p. 111.
403 See also: B.H.W., at: Knecht des Heren (Servant of the Lord).
404 B.H.W., at: Slaaf (Slave); Van den Born, 1969-1969, at: Dienaar (Servant).
405 Abdus Sattar, 2003, p. 98.
406 Attema, 1962, p. 75-77.
407 Wessels, 2006, p. 83.
408 Attema, 1962, p. 47.
409 Ayoeb, 2005, p. 52-53.
410 Laffin, 1976, p. 38; Abdus Sattar, 2003, p. 94. Contra-information from a
     later date is not known to me.
411 Beck, 2002, p. 66 e.v.
412 Beck, 2002, p. 66-70, renders that modern Islamic scholars sometimes
     omit this sixth principle of faith about predestination.
413 Attema , 1962, p. 6.
414 See for a vivid explanation in Dutch about these affairs e.g.: Attema,
     1962, p. 53-64.
415 See also the discussions in: Attema, 1962, p. 147-166; Wessels, 2006, p. 79
     e.v.
416 Wessels, 2006, p. 79.
417 Abdus Sattar, 2003, p. 47-48.
418 Attema, 1962, p. 44-45.
419 Wessels, 2006, p. 86-89.
420 Karagül, 1996, p. 38, 54.

421 In the word register of Kramer's Koran translation in the Dutch language (1974, p. 718) this is finely demonstrated. In many cases where English translations have "peace", Kramer translates more correctly "mutual agreement" (Dutch: "schikking") (e.g. Sura 2:224).

422 Laffin, 1976, p. 17.

423 Abdus Sattar, 2003, p. 24.

424 Karagül, 1996, p. 38.

425 Karagül, 1996, p. 40-41.

426 Karagül, 1996, p. 45.

427 Laffin, 1976, p. 29.

428 Wessels, 2006, p. 134.

429 Attema, 1962, p. 88-92.

430 Attema, 1962, p. 93.

431 See e.g.: Katsh, 1962, passim.

432 Wessels, 2006, p. 130.

433 Abdus Sattar, 2003, p. 19-20.

434 In the Pickthal translation (see e.g.
http://www.searchtruth.com/chapter_
display.php?chapter=1&translator=4) the words "stranger" and "foreigner" are missing completely. In the Mohsin Khan translation (see: http://
www.searchtruth.com/chapter_display.php?chapter=1&translator=5) "stranger" only appears in Sura 4:36 and 15:70, "foreigner" only in Sura 15:70. The use of these words in this translation is a broadening interpretation at this point. Pickthal translates Sura 4:36 more in line with the original: "the neighbour who is not of kin" instead of "a stranger" (meant is someone who could be one of your people but doesn't belong to your family). Sura 15:70 is translated by Pickthal with: "anyone" instead of "people, foreigners and strangers from us". This Sura tells the story of Lut (Hebrew: Lot) and doesn't contain a religious command.

435 Wynia, 2005.

436 Bartels, 1995, p. 24-25.

437 Bartels, 1995, p. 21.

438 Bartels, 1995, p. 51.

439 Bartels, 1995, p. 54.

440 Bartels, 1995, p. 69.

441 Bartels, 1995, p. 73.

442 Bartels, 1995, p. 75.

443 De Vries, 1995, p. 25-26.

444 De Vries, 1995, p. 25.

445 Discourses on the history of philosophy pay hardly any attention to this aspect of Descartes' thought. I found these four virtues on a website of students of the Open University.

446 De Vries, 1995, p. 31-32.

447 Hooykaas, 1979, p. 221.

448 Hooykaas, 1979, p. 216.

449 Daalderop, 2006.

450 De Vries, 1995, p. 33.

451 So Friedriech Engels in: Herr Eugen Dührings Umwälzung der Wissenschaft, 1878 (see: E.B.Mac., at: Marxism).

452 De Vries, 1995, p. 35.

453 Buruma, 2004, p. 37.

454 Buruma, 2004, p. 37-38.

455 Buruma, 2004, p. 78.

456 Buruma, 2004, p. 79-80.

457 Buruma, 2004, p. 51.

458 Buruma, 2004, p. 5.

459 Buruma, 2004, p. 77.

460 Buruma, 2004, p. 51.

461 The next paragraphs are mainly based on: Stein, 2005.

462 Van 't Riet, 2001, p. 10.

Literature

English literature

ARN = Avot de Rabbi Nathan (*Goldin, 1967*)

Ayoub, M.M., *Islam, Faith and History*, Oxford, 2005, 2e druk

Braude, W.G. (Ed.), *The Midrash on Psalms*, Translated from the Hebrew, 2 Vol., New Haven, 1959

Bunim, I.M., *Ethics from Sinai, A wide-ranging commentary on Pirkei Avos*, 3 Vol., Jerusalem/New York, 2000

Buruma, I., Margalit, A., *Occidentalism, The West in the Eyes of its Enemies*, New York, 2004

E.B. Mac. = *Encyclopaedia Britannica*, Macropaedia, 15th Edition, Chicago, 1979

E.B. Mic. = *Encyclopaedia Britannica*, Micropaedia, 15th Edition, Chicago, 1979

E.J. = *Encyclopaedia Judaica*, Jerusalem, 1978

Freedman, H., Simon, M., *Midrash Rabbah, Translated into English with notes, glossary and indices*, 10 Delen, Londen, 1961, 3e druk

Ginzberg, L., *The legends of the Jews*, 7 Volumes, Philadelphia, 1968-1969

Glatzer, N.N., *Hillel the Elder, The emergence of Classical Judaism*, New York, 1966

Goldin, J., *The living Talmud, The Wisdom of the Fathers*, New York, 1957

Goldin, J., *The Fathers according to Rabbi Nathan*, Translated from the Hebrew by J. Goldin, London, 1967, 3e druk

Hertz, J.H., *The authorised Daily Prayer Book*, Hebrew text, English translation with commentary and notes, Revised edition, London/Jerusalem/New York, 1976

Heschel, A.J., *Man's quest for God, Studies in prayer and symbolism*, New York, 1954

Hirsch, S.R., The Hirsch Siddur, *The Order of Prayer for the whole Year*, Jerusalem/New York, 1978

Katsh, A.I., *Judaism and the Koran, Biblical and talmudical backgrounds of the Koran and its commentaties*, New York, 1962, 2e druk

Lauterbach, J.Z., *Mekilta de-Rabbi Ishmael*, Critical edition on the basis of the manuscripts and early editions, English translation, introduction and notes, 3 Vol., Philadelphia, 1976

Maimonides, *Mishneh Torah, Maimonides' Code of Law and Ethics*, Annotated with an introduction bij Philip Birnbaum, New York, 1974, 3e druk

Millgram, A., *Jewish worship*, Philadelphia, USA, 1975, 2e druk

LITERATURE

Musaph-Andriesse, R. C., *From Torah to Kabbalah: A Basic Introduction to the Writings of Judaism*, Oxford University Press, USA, 1982

Neusner, *Invitation to the Talmud*, A teaching book, New York, 1975, 2e druk

NKJV = New King James Bible

Pedersen, J., *Israel, its life and culture*, Volumes I-II, Londen/Kopenhagen, 1926

Rashi, Sapirstein Edition, *The Torah with Rashi's Commentary Translated, Annotated and Elucidated*, Vols. 1-5, Editor: Rabbi Yisrael Herczeg, Mesorah Publications, New York

Riet, P. van 't, *Reading Torah, The Key to the Gospels*, E-book Edition, Folianti, Zwolle, 2012; Paperback Edition, Kampen, 2018.

T.D.O.T. = *Theological Dictionary of the Old Testament*, G.J. Botterweck and H. Ringgren (Ed.), Grand Rapids, 1977, 2e druk

Travers Herford, R., *The Ethics of the Talmud: Sayings of the Fathers*, New York, 1969, 5e druk

Urbach, E.E., The Sages, *Their concepts and beliefs*, 2 Vol., Jerusalem, 1979

German literature

Buber, M., Rosenzweig, F., *Die Fünf Bücher der Weisung*, Köln/Olten, 1954

E.E.K. = *Evangelischer Erwachsenen Katechismus, Kursbuch des Glaubens, Im Auftrag der Katechismuskommission der Vereinigten Evangelisch-Lutherischen Kirche Deutschlands*, Gütersloh, 1977

Gesenius, W., *Hebräisches und aramäisches Handwörterbuch über das Alte Testament*, Berlin/Göttingen/Heidelberg, 1962, 17e druk

Goldschmidt, L., *Der Babylonische Talmud*, 12 Bände, Berlin, 1964-1967, 2e druk

Köhler, H., *Theologische Anthropologie, Die biblische Sicht des Menschen und der Mensch in der Gegenwart*, München, 1967

Lehmann, M., *Sprüche der Väter*, 3 Bände, Basel, 1963

Mayer, R., (Ed.), *Der Talmud, Ausgewählt, übersetzt und erklärt*, München, 1980, 5e druk

R.u.T. = *Taschenlexikon Religion und Theologie*, 4 Delen, E. Herdieckerhoff, J. Tolk (Red.), Göttingen, 1971

Strack, H.L., Billerbeck, P., *Kommentar zum Neuen Testament aus Talmud und Midrasch*, 6 Bände, München, 1969, 5e druk

Weber, O., *Grundlagen der Dogmatik I*, Neukirchen, 1987

Dutch literature

Abdus Sattar, S., *Islam voor beginners, Een heldere inleiding tot de wereld van de Islam*, Amsterdam, 2003, 4e druk

LITERATURE

Abram, I.B.H., *Joodse traditie als permanent leren*, B. Folkertsma Stichting voor Talmudica, 1980

Aschkenasy, Y., Tomson, P.J., Uden, D.J. van, Whitlau, W.A.C., *Geliefd is de mens*, Hilversum, 1981

Aschkenasy, Y., Whitlau, E., Loopik, M. van, Marx, Tz. (Red.), *Tenachon, Over bijbelse en rabbijnse concepten*, Hilversum, 2001-2002

Aschkenasy, Y., Whitlau, W.A.C., Geliefd is de mens, Over een spreuk van Rabbi Akiba (Avoth III, 14), in: *Aschkenasy e.a., 1981*, pag. 7-24

Attema, D.S., *De Koran, Zijn ontstaan en zijn inhoud*, Kampen, 1962

B.H.W. = *Reicke & Rost, 1969-1970*

Barnard, W.J., Riet, P. van 't, *Zonder Tora leest niemand wel, Bouwstenen voor een leeswijze van de evangeliën gebaseerd op Tenach en joodse traditie*, Kampen, 1986

Barnard, W.J., Riet, P. van 't, *De slip van een joodse man vastgrijpen, Christelijke eredienst in het spoor van de joodse Jezus*, Kampen, 1989

Bartels, J., *De geschiedenis van het subject, Descartes, Spinoza, Kant*, Kampen, 1995, 2e druk

Beck, H., *Islam in hoofdlijnen*, Zoetermeer, 2002

Beentjes, P., *Jesus, zoon van Sirach*, Averbode, 1982

Benima, T.M., Bommel, A. van, Karagül, A., Meijers, L.D., Reinders, J.S., Vroom, H.M., Wessels, A., *Heilige Schriften, waarden en plurale samenleving*, Kampen, 1996

Berkhof, H., *De mens onderweg, Een christelijke mensbeschouwing*, 's-Gravenhage, 1976

Berkhof, H., *Christelijk geloof, Een inleiding tot de geloofsleer*, Nijkerk, z.j., 4e druk

Boertien, M., *Het joodse leerhuis van 200 voor tot 200 na Christus*, Kampen, 1974

Born, A. van den (Red.), *Bijbels Woordenboek*, Romen's Woordenboeken, Roermond, 1966-1969, 3e druk

Boxel, P.W. van, *De Wijsheid van de Vaderen*, Het Misjnatractaat Avot vertaald en toegelicht, Kampen, 1994

Brienen, T., *Leren in Jodendom en Christendom, De plaats van Israël in de Catechetiek*, Kampen, 1990

Bruin, T. de (Red.), *Adam waar ben je?, De betekenis van het mensbeeld in de joodse traditie en in de psychotherapie*, Hilversum, 1983

Buber, M., *Chassidische vertellingen*, Katwijk, 1967, 3e druk

C.E. (1) = *Christelijke Encyclopaedie voor het Nederlandsche volk*, F.W. Grosheide, J.H. Landwehr, C. Lindeboom, J.C. Rullmann (Red.), Kampen, 1925-1931

C.E. (2) = *Christelijke Encyclopedie*, F.W. Grosheide, G.P. van Itterzon (Red.), Kampen, 1956-1961

Daalderop, K., Freud bleef trouw aan zijn wortels, in: *Trouw*, 2006 (6 mei)

LITERATURE

Dasberg, J. (Vert.), *Siach Jitschak, Gebed van Jitschak, Siddoer, De geordende gebeden voor het gehele jaar*, Jeruzalem/Amsterdam, 1977

Deen, R., De pedagogiek van het Sjema, Over het verband tussen bidden en leren, in: *De Kwaadsteniet en De Wilde, 1990*, pag. 37-48

Evers, R., *Tijd van leven, De Bijbel tegen de 24-uurseconomie*, Kampen, 1998

Evers, R., Sidra van de week, Pinchas (Bemidbar/Numeri 25:10 - 30:1), in: *NIW*, 2006 (14 juli), pag. 31

Hausdorff, D., Inleiding op de Tefilla, in: *Dasberg (Siach Jitschak), 1977*, pag. IV-XXIII

Herzberg, A., *Amor Fati*. Querido, Amsterdam, 1977.

Heyer, C.J. den, *De Messiaanse weg, Deel 1, Messiaanse verwachtingen in het Oude Testament en in de vroeg-joodse traditie*, Kampen, 1983

Hooykaas, R., *Geschiedenis der natuurwetenschappen, Van Babel tot Bohr*, Utrecht, 1979, 2e druk

Karagül, A., Hoe lezen moslims hun heilige schrift: de Qur'an, in: *Benima e.a.*, 1996, pag. 37-55

Klein, T., Synode: 'Jezus is Zoon van God', Overgrote meerderheid stemt in met belijdend geschrift over Jezus, in: *Centraal Weekblad*, 2000 (8 december), pag. 7

Kramers, J.H., *De Koran, Uit het Arabisch vertaald*, Amsterdam, 1974, 4e druk

Kuitert, H.M., *De realiteit van het geloof, Over de anti-metafysische tendens in de huidige theologische ontwikkeling*, Kampen, 1971

Kushner, H.S., *Op het leven!, Een loflied op het joodse leven en denken*, Baarn, 1993

Kwaadsteniet, J. de, Wilde, N. de, (Red.), *Veel liefde hebt U ons bewezen, Een commentaar bij het Sjema Israël*, Hilversum, 1990

Laffin, J., *De Arabische mentaliteit, Aspecten van een onbegrepen cultuur*, Utrecht/Antwerpen, 1976

Lapide, P., *Hij leerde in hun synagogen, Een joodse uitleg van de evangeliën*, Baarn, 1983

Lepper, J.L.M. de, *De godsdienst der Romeinen*, Roermond/Maaseik, 1950

Levinas, E., *Het menselijk gelaat*, Baarn, 1969

Loopik, M. van, *De wegen der wijzen en de weg van de wereld*, Kampen, 1989

Maarsen, I., *De Spreuken der Vaderen*, Vertaald, verklaard en van een inleiding voorzien, Zutphen, 1932

Meer, F. van der, *Lofzangen der Latijnse Kerk*, Utrecht/Antwerpen, 1970

Musaph-Andriesse, *Wat na de Tora kwam, Rabbijnse literatuur van Tora tot Kabbala*, Baarn, 1973

N.K. = *De Nieuwe Katechismus, Geloofsverkondiging voor volwassenen*, In opdracht van de bisschoppen van Nederland, Hilversum, 1966

NIW = *Nieuw Israëlietisch Weekblad*, Amsterdam

LITERATURE

O.v.D. = *Orden van dienst en Heidelbergse Catechismus voor gebruik in de eredienst van de Gereformeerde Kerken in Nederland*, Samengesteld door Deputaten voor de Eredienst, 1973

Onderwijzer, A.S., *Nederlandsche vertaling van den Pentateuch benevens eene Nederlandsche vertaling van Rashie's Pentateuch-Commentaar*, 5 Delen, Amsterdam, 1977, 2e druk

Palache, J.L., *Inleiding in de Talmoed*, Amstelveen, 1984, 4e druk

Peli, P.H., Weet tegenover wie je staat, Enkele facetten van het joodse gebed, in: *Verkenning en Bezinning*, 1988

Petuchowski, J.J., *Aan Uw erbarmen is geen einde, Joodse gebeden*, Baarn, 1987

Polak, G.I., Mulder, S.I., *Volledig Dagelijksch Gebedenboek der Nederlandsche Israëliten voor het gehele Jaar*, Amsterdam, 1862, 5e druk

Prijs, L., *Inleiding in de joodse godsdienst*, Kampen, 1980

Riet, P. van 't, *Het evangelie uit het leerhuis van Lazarus, Een speurtocht naar de joodse herkomst van het vierde evangelie*, Baarn, 1996

Riet, P. van 't, *Christendom à la Jezus, De herziening van het christelijk geloof vanuit haar joodse bronnen*, Kampen, 2001

Rosen, J., *De Talmoed en het internet, Een reis tussen werelden*, Amsterdam/Antwerpen, 2001

S.V. = *Statenvertaling* : Bijbel, Dat is de Gansche Heilige Schrift bevattende al de Canonieke Boeken des Ouden Testaments, Door last van de Hoog-Mogende Heeren Staten-Generaal der Vereenigde Nederlanden etc.

Scheepstra, S.E., *Het Leerhuis, Aspecten van het onderwijs in het klassieke jodendom*, Kampen, 1983

Schelling, P., Sjalom, veelkleurig bijbels sleutelwoord, in: *Interpretatie*, 2002, pag. 15-17

Sluis, D.J. van der, Tomson, P.J., Uden, D.J. van, Whitlau, W.A.C., *Elke morgen nieuw, Inleiding tot de Joodse gedachtewereld aan de hand van het Achttiengebed*, B. Folkertsma Stichting voor Talmudica, 1978

Soetendorp, J., *Symboliek der joodse religie, Beschrijving en verklaring der gebruiken in het joodse leven*, Zeist, 1953

Stein, Y., 'Ik beschrijf hoe mensen echt zijn', Interview met Theodore Dalrymple, in: *Trouw*, 2005 (14 november)

Tijn, M. van, *Een historische inleiding op de Misjna, Vrede! Er is geen vrede*, 's-Gravenhage, 1988

Uden, D.J. van, Gezegend Gij Heer, Over bidden en gebed in de joodse traditie, in: *Verkenning en bezinning*, 1978

V&B = *Verkenning en bezinning*, Reeks geschriften over de verhouding van de kerk en het Joodse volk, Kampen

LITERATURE

Vreekamp, H., In het beeld van God : Over de verhouding van God en mens in jodendom en Christendom. In: *Zicht op Israël II : Voortgaande reformatorische bezinning op de verhouding van Kerk en Israël in bijbels perspectief.* C. den Boer, M. van Campen, J. van der Graaf (Ed.). Den Haag, 1987.

Vries, G. de, *De ontwikkeling van de wetenschap, Een inleiding in de wetenschapsfilosofie,* Groningen, 1995, 3e druk

Vries, S.Ph. de, *Joodse riten en symbolen,* Amsterdam, 1968, 4e druk

Wegman, H.A.J., *Geschiedenis van de Christelijke eredienst in het Westen en in het Oosten,* Een wegwijzer, Hilversum, 1983

Wessels, *De Koran verstaan,* Kampen, 2006, 6e druk

Wiesel, E, *Bijbels eerbetoon, Portretten en legenden,* Hilversum, 1976

Wynia, S., Succesvol mensbeeld, in: *Elsevier,* 2005 (29 October), pag. 16-17

About the author

Dr. S.P. (Peter) van 't Riet (1948) studied studied mathematics and psychology at the Free University of Amsterdam and wrote his thesis on an educational-psychological subject. He was successively a teacher of mathematics at a school for secundary education, teacher of the didactics of mathematics at the Technical University of Delft, manager at the Teacher Training Centre of Zwolle, director and professor at the Windesheim University of Zwolle.

Since the seventies he has studied the Judaism of the first centuries as well as the Jewish exegesis of the Bible, especially the Jewish character of the New Testament. He published the following titles in Dutch (the first four together with his fellow-author Will J. Barnard):

- Luke, the Jew (1984)
- Reading Tora, the Key to the Gospels (1986)
- As a Dove to the Land of Assur (1988)
- Catching the Coat-tail of a Jewish Man (1989)
- The Gospel from the Study-house of Lazarus (1996)
- Luke, the Jew (2ᵉ revised edition, 1997)
- Christianity à la Jesus (2001)
- Luke versus Matthew (2005)
- The Image of Man in the Torah (2006)
- The Philosophy of the Creation-story (2008)
- Luke, the Jew (3ᵉ revised edition, 2009)
- Reading Tora, the Key to the Gospels (2ᵉ revised edition, 2010)

In 2012 two English translation were published as e-books: *Reading Tora, the Key to the Gospels* and *Luke, the Jew,* in 2014 followed by *The Image of Man in the Tora* and in 2018 by *A Dove to the Land of War*. These four titles are also for sale as paperback editions on Amazon.com. More information about these and other publications of the author can be found on his website: www.petervantriet.nl.